What two key Christian leaders say about *Miracles:*

Dr. John MacArthur:

> I have read with deep appreciation virtually every book Dr. Morris has written since his landmark book, *The Genesis Flood.* His knowledge of both science and Scripture makes everything he writes a treasure, and his uncompromising defense of biblical creationism has been of immense value to all who love the Word of God. Now he has given us a superb study of miracles from the perspective of a scientist and a believer.

Dr. MacArthur is pastor of Grace Community Church in Sun Valley, California. He has written many widely appreciated books, and hosts the nationwide "Grace to You" radio program. He also serves as president of Master's College and Seminary.

Dr. David Jeremiah:

> *Miracles* combines an intimately personal, poignant, and profound insight into this complex issue — I am honored to recommend this book. I have enjoyed reading it and have learned from it. As you read it, I am confident that God will bless and enrich your life [from the foreword].

Dr. Jeremiah is senior pastor of Shadow Mountain Community Church (Southern Baptist) of El Cajon, California, and main speaker on the popular nationwide television and radio program "Turning Point." He is also serving as chancellor of Christian Heritage College, and has authored a number of best-selling books.

Miracles

Miracles

Do They Still Happen?
Why We Believe Them.

Henry M. Morris

Master
Books

First printing: January 2004

ISBN: 0-89051-413-5

Library of Congress Number: 2003116025

Printed in the United States of America

Please visit our website for other great titles:
www.masterbooks.net

For information regarding author interviews,
please contact the publicity department at (870) 438-5288.

ACKNOWLEDGMENTS

Drs. John Morris and Henry Morris III, my two sons, both read and critiqued the manuscript for *Miracles* and made a number of helpful suggestions. In addition, my daughter, Mary Ruth Smith, typed and edited it.

I am especially grateful to Dr. John MacArthur and Dr. David Jeremiah, both of whom have also read the complete manuscript. These are two of this generation's most eminent evangelical writers and Bible teachers, and I am thankful for their interest and approval. Dr. Jeremiah, who is pastor of the church where I have been a member for over 33 years, has graciously prepared a brief foreword for the book, and Dr. MacArthur has also written a very kind endorsement.

Then, of course, there are Jim Fletcher and his associates on the editorial staff at Master Books, who did the final editing and preparation for publication. I appreciate the fine work of all these talented and gracious people.

Contents

Foreword

Do *miracles really happen?* The answer to that question comes uniquely packaged in this book through Dr. Henry Morris's intellect as a scientist and his passion for God's Word. *Miracles* combines an intimately personal, poignant, and profound insight into this complex issue. You will profit from its pages.

What about science? Doesn't our modern knowledge refute the supernatural? Dr. Morris's resounding "no" to the skepticism of our day is backed up by his 60-year ministry among the scientific elite of our world. The powerful signature of our Creator God is written large throughout the universe. The laws of His cosmos, reinforced by the record of His Word, testify to the reality of God and His supernatural intervention into the affairs of men.

How do we know when God performs a miracle? The Bible teaches us that Satan can counterfeit much and can masquerade as an "angel of light." How can we tell a "real" miracle from a false one? Dr. Morris's very practical presentation of Grade A, B, and C real miracles is a special blessing in this book. That analysis, and the biblical and scientific foundations on which it is based, makes this discussion a valuable resource for student and scholar alike.

What are the unique miracles that only a Creator God can perform? The founding miracles of the primeval age are the absolute boundaries of a biblical world view. The seven great miracles of Jesus Christ recorded in John's gospel are recorded "that you might believe that Jesus is the Christ, the Son of God" (John 20:31). Dr. Morris explains and clarifies their role in our thinking as he sets the stage for their application to our lives.

I am honored to recommend this book. I have enjoyed reading it and have learned from it. As you read it, I am confident that God will bless and enrich your own life.

— Dr. David Jeremiah

Introduction

A number of Christian authors have written books on the subject of miracles, and it would be reasonable to ask why I should write one. I was reluctant to do this, since I tend to be very skeptical about alleged modern miracles anyway.

However, my son, Dr. John Morris, having heard me speak on this subject once or twice, had been urging me to write a small book on miracles, so I had been considering it. Just yesterday, an incident occurred which helped me to decide.

Miracles

The event was an auto accident, which totaled my car. I had been very fond of my Buick, having purchased it new in 1989 and driven it ever since. Also, I was somewhat smug about my driving record, having been driving ever since 1936 without ever being involved in an accident.

Well, no longer! Yesterday was a rainy day (rare in San Diego!) and my wife and I were starting up a long hill when a car coming fast down that hill skidded and crashed hard into the door on the driver's side. The whole left side of my Buick was a shambles.

Except that, no glass was broken, and neither Mary Louise nor I were injured. That seemed miraculous enough for me to decide to go ahead with a study of miracles. Whether it was really the Lord speaking to me or not (actually, I had been praying for some sort of indication), I guess time will tell. Anyway, here goes!

And the man of God said, Where fell it?
And he shewed him the place. And he cut
down a stick, and cast it in thither;
and the iron did swim.

(2 Kings 6:6)

STUDY THE SCIENCES IN THE LIGHT OF THE TRUTH,
THAT IS — AS BEFORE GOD; FOR THEIR BUSINESS IS TO
SHOW THE TRUTH, THAT IS TO SAY, GOD EVERYWHERE.
WRITE NOTHING, SAY NOTHING, THINK NOTHING
THAT YOU CANNOT BELIEVE TO BE TRUE BEFORE GOD.

— JOSEPH JOUBERT, 1754–1824

CHAPTER I

Miracles and the Scientists

There is no doubt that the scientific establishment, and intellectuals in general, have long declared that miracles are impossible. But it is also true that the Bible describes many true miracles that really did happen. There are also many people, especially among both occultists and charismatic evangelicals, who claim real miracles occur fairly often today, but most people have been skeptical about these claims.

However, I have personally received what I believe to be many wonderful answers to prayer, sometimes in ways that could almost be described as miraculous. So the subject seems definitely worth exploring. Exactly what *is* a real miracle, do they occur today, and (if they do) under what conditions? Furthermore, many of the Bible miracles seem to be truly supernatural, but just how good is the evidence that they really happened?

A somewhat formal chapter on miracles is already available in one of my books (*The Biblical Basis for Modern Science*), but the discussion in this little book will be somewhat less formal, and will include a number of personal testimonies. For any who wish to look into this subject in greater depth, there are a few books listed in the bibliographic section at the end that will be helpful.

But before we try to decide whether real miracles have ever occurred, either past or present, we need to define them first of all. If we say they are phenomena which occur outside the laws of science, then we need to understand what really are the laws of science. Obviously, real miracles are rare; otherwise they would be of little interest and could probably be explained scientifically.

Therefore, I shall try to explain in the next four chapters exactly what these natural laws and processes that we call science do and do not tell us. Then we can probably define a real miracle, rather informally, as an event which is impossible scientifically, but which happens anyway. The evidence for such therefore cannot be found in science itself, but in terms of testimony and personal observation and will depend largely on the credibility of the witnesses.

But then there are also many events which do not seem to be contradicting any scientific laws as such but which do seem to go beyond the laws of probability. These are often regarded as special answers to prayer or, perhaps, as special indicators of God's leading. Are we justified in regarding such instances as miraculous? I think so. Even though they have not required supernatural suspension of any basic scientific law, they often seem so clearly to be answers to prayer, and so unlikely in any ordinary course of events, that we can certainly consider them providential, at least, and so why not call them, say, providential miracles?

Afghanistan and God's Providence

For example, one of the key "miracles" of that sort in my own life occurred many years ago (about 1949) when I was teaching civil engineering and also working on my Ph.D. degree in hydraulics at the University of Minnesota. I was also preparing to go to Afghanistan as a so-called non-professional missionary. Plans were under way to develop an engineering college in Kabul, and I was scheduled to be head of its civil engineering department. The Afghan government had approved this college as a project to be staffed by Americans and equipped by donations from American companies.

Afghanistan is very much in the news in recent years, but at that time few Americans knew anything about it, except that its culture and living standards were inferior to those in America, to put it mildly. There had been no engineering school in the entire nation, and very little education of any kind. As a totally Muslim nation, Christian missionaries were not even permitted to enter the country, and the people were forbidden to have Bibles or to consider Christianity at all, on penalty of death.

But the secular leaders of Afghanistan (its king and others) were beginning to see the need of technological development of the country, and so gave their okay to the proposed engineering college. The instigator of that project had been a young Christian named Dick Soderberg who, though a well-educated American engineer himself, had gone as a non-professional missionary to teach in the single Kabul high school. He was able to witness surreptitiously to Muslims here and there and even to lead a small number to Christ, though they were in mortal danger if discovered.

He saw the desperate need in Afghanistan of an engineering school, and also the possibilities of recruiting genuine Christians as its teachers. I was one of his recruits. Gordon Van Wylen (then studying at MIT but destined later to become dean of engineering at Michigan University), and Christy Wilson Jr. (son of a veteran missionary to Iran and later destined to organize Kabul's first Christian church — only for foreigners, however) were others. And, of course, I was another. The entire faculty had been recruited by 1949, along with many promises of equipment and funds. I even recruited one of my own students in civil engineering, Bob Knutson, to go as a lab instructor.

But I needed first to finish my own Ph.D. work. It had gone well, and all I had left was to finish the dissertation. However, I had somehow developed a hernia, and the doctors insisted that, in view of the primitive medical facilities in Afghanistan, I should have an operation before leaving the States. Since I was also teaching a full load of courses at the university, it seemed the only time available would be the Christmas holidays, but that was the time I had planned to use to complete the dissertation.

At the insistence of the doctors, however, I did check into the hospital one evening, with the surgery scheduled for the next morning. When the nurse came around that evening for routine preparation, she found that I had developed a significant fever. They could not operate with that condition, so they sent me home.

My wife, Mary Louise, who had worked before our marriage as a doctor's assistant, then checked my temperature at home, and it was back to normal. So early next morning, I saw the doctor at his office, but once again had a fever. Therefore, they decided I should wait several days before going ahead with the operation.

All of that meant I could devote full-time to finishing my dissertation, which I proceeded to do, finally receiving the Ph.D. in good time to proceed with our plans for Afghanistan. We already had our equipment and everything else in readiness but, at that juncture, the Afghan government suddenly reneged on the proposed engineering college, so we never got there after all.

I concluded that the Lord wanted us to be *willing* to go on a difficult and possibly dangerous mission like that, but — knowing I would probably make a very poor missionary — never really intended us *actually* to go. We had five children at the time, with another on the way, and it certainly would have made things different in their — later quite fruitful — lives as well.

But to further clinch the case that all this was a sort of protracted providential miracle, that was over 50 years ago, and I never did get around to that operation! In fact, every physical exam since that time has shown no evidence of the hernia at all!

There have been one or two other providential miracles of that kind in my life, and I'll mention these later. There was no evidence of any supernatural process, of course, and I think most active Christians could also testify to answers to prayer in their own lives of this sort. I feel comfortable in calling them miracles — miracles of providential leading and ordering of circumstances. Perhaps they work more slowly than an instantaneous turning of water into wine, say, but just as effectively in the long run, as God proceeds to work all things *"together for good to them that love God, to them who are the called according to His purpose"* (Rom. 8:28).

But what about true supernatural miracles, such as, say, the raising of Lazarus after four days in the grave or Elijah calling fire down from heaven on Mount Carmel? And exactly what and where is the dividing line between such supernatural miracles and providential miracles? The Bible does, indeed, record many miracles requiring supernatural intervention in scientific laws — such as, say, God enabling Balaam's ass to speak in human language to Balaam — but it also describes many apparently providential miracles — such as, say, the remarkable timing of the Philippian earthquake to get Paul and Silas out of prison.

Do real supernatural miracles still occur today, and how would we recognize them if they do?

Such questions require a more precise definition of scientific laws and processes, for one thing, and also a closer look at the various miracles in the Bible, in comparison to modern answers to prayer and also to modern *claims* of the supernatural. We do know that our Lord Jesus Christ is *"the same yesterday, and to day, and for ever"* (Heb. 13:8), so that true miracles of both kinds are certainly possible. But we also must not forget, especially in what may well turn out to be the last days, that Christ warned of the coming of *"false prophets"* and even *"false Christs,"* who would be able to show *"great signs, and wonders"* that might deceive, *"if it were possible,* [even] *the very elect"* (Matt. 24:24).

Fair weather cometh out of the north:

with God is terrible majesty.

(Job 37:22)

I SAW THE LIGHTNING'S GLEAMING ROD

REACH FORTH AND WRITE UPON THE SKY

THE AWFUL AUTOGRAPH OF GOD.

— JOAQUIN MILLER

CHAPTER II

The Nature of Natural Processes

B efore we can effectively classify or evaluate any miraculous interventions in natural laws or processes, we need to understand just what those laws and processes are. Where did *they* come from, and how did the scientific establishment determine their actions and limitations?

There are innumerable natural (and artificial) processes functioning in the world. Scientists have tried to organize their study of these processes into different categories — biological processes, chemical processes, physical processes, etc. The disciplines in which they are studied are correspondingly called biology, chemistry, physics, and so on, with many subdivisions and combinations — geology, hydrology, physiology, astronomy, etc. — as well as biochemistry, geophysics, paleobiology, and on and on ad infinitum.

So one group of scientists will study the natural flow of water down a river channel, another the artificial process of petrochemicals driving man-made machines such as automobiles, and another the phenomena of metabolism in living organisms. The number and variety seem endless.

The Tri-universe

But the remarkable unifying factor about all this is that they all function in a *universe* (not a polyverse) of space, time, and matter. Thus they must somehow be described in terms of the space they occupy (measured in terms of feet, square feet or cubic feet, or the corresponding dimensions in the metric system, or whatever), the time during which they function (measured usually in seconds or hours or years) and the material phenomena involved in this space-time framework. The latter are measured in terms of mass and forces operating on the mass.

There are a number of different types of force in the universe — gravity, tension, compression, friction, nuclear, electricity, chemical, elasticity, etc. — and their magnitudes are commonly measured in terms of pounds, at least in our English system. This English system, therefore, is commonly called the foot-pound-second system, and thus all processes ultimately involve just these three dimensions, or combinations thereof.

Furthermore, the very concept of "process" involves something happening in terms of movement, interchange of forces, or both, all in a framework involving space, time, and matter (or force acting in or on matter). Another very interesting fact then appears. The universe in which all these processes function is a space/time/matter universe, but it is not "divided" into these three components — part space, part time, part matter. Rather it is all space, all time, and all phenomena of matter occurring in space and time.

Thus the universe is actually a remarkable "tri-universe," only capable of existing in terms of three components, each of which is the whole. One then immediately thinks of the divine Trinity — Father, Son, and Holy Spirit — each of which is fully and perfectly God. Each is a distinct person, but comprising only one God. The analogy seems so striking and fitting that there must be more than coincidence involved. That is, the tri-universe seems to be a good model of the triune godhead.

In a sense, therefore, all the processes of the universe testify of their Creator, operating as they do in a dimensional structure that remarkably "models" His own "structure." No wonder the use of models and dimensional analysis has become such a powerful tool in scientific research. The scientist can build a small-scale model of the process he is studying, make his measurements of the forces and motions involved on the model, then extrapolate to the full-scale phenomenon, using the principles of dimensional analysis in this triune framework to formulate his equations or descriptions of the prototype. The model can be an actual small-scale physical model of the prototype or a computer model, or even a thought model, and these principles must apply. Whether he knows it or not (and usually

such an idea never enters his mind), the scientist is unintentionally using this testimony to the nature of God as he tries to formulate an equation or description of the phenomenon without any acknowledgement to God in his results.

The Laws of Thermodynamics

Another very remarkable and important feature common to all natural processes has emerged from their scientific study. That is, all processes — whether physical, chemical, biological, or any other — are found to operate within two basic universal laws. One is the law of conservation in quantity, the other the law of decay of quality. That is, whatever force or energy phenomena are occurring in the process, the total always is conserved — there is neither creation of new matter nor annihilation of existing matter (or force or energy) taking place. However, the availability and usefulness of the energies in the process always tends to decrease.

These two principles (conservation of energy quantity and decay of energy availability) are also called the first and second laws of thermodynamics, and they are certainly the best proved and most universally applicable of all natural laws. All processes operate within their constraints, although they were first recognized and quantified in connection with the development of the steam engine, when engineers found that the force of steam could generate motion of vehicles. Hence the name — "laws of thermodynamics." It was soon realized, however, that they were fully applicable to all manner of forces, processes, and systems.

Practically all processes, whether physical or biological or anything else, involve interchange and exchange of energy, and these interchanges always obey the two laws of thermodynamics. As the great Harvard physicist P. W. Bridgman said many years ago, "The two laws of thermodynamics are, I suppose, accepted by physicists as perhaps the most secure generalizations from experience that we have" (*American Scientist*, October 1953, p. 549).

Another great physicist of the same generation, Dr. R.B. Lindsay, dean of the graduate school at Brown University, wrote concerning the basic importance of the concept of energy to science as follows.

> Of all unifying concepts in the whole field of physical science, that of energy has proved to be the most significant and useful. Not only has it played a major role in the logical development of the structure of science, but, by common consent, it is the physical concept which has had and still has the widest influence on human life in all its aspects. . . . the interpretation of phenomena in terms of the transfer of energy between natural systems is the most powerful single tool in the understanding of the external world (*Scientific Monthly*, October 1957, p. 188).

Although these comments by two great physicists were published a half century ago, they are still as true as ever.

As far as the universal validity of the two laws of thermodynamics is concerned, the following more recent comments may be noted from two leading modern physicists.

> The first law of thermodynamics . . . states that all energy in the universe is constant — that is, the sum of

all energy is fixed, has been fixed since the beginning of time, and will remain so until the end of time. . . . Even so, energy can appear in various forms, for example, heat, light, gravitation, invisible radiation, kinetic energy, mechanical work, chemical potential, nuclear energy, and so forth; matter itself is a form of energy. Furthermore, the many varied forms of energy can be interchanged, including matter transforming into energy. . . . In short, the first law of thermodynamics decrees that energy itself can be neither created nor destroyed, though its many forms can change (Eric J. Chaisson, *Cosmic Evolution*, Harvard University Press, 2001, p. 16).

No exception to the second law of thermodynamics has ever been found — not even a tiny one. . . . As Albert Einstein put it, "It is the only physical theory of universal content that . . . will never be overthrown" (Elliott H. Lieb and Jakob Yngvason, *Physics Today*, April 2000, p. 32).

Therefore, we are on solid footing if we recognize these two laws as *the* laws of science which an event would have to overcome if it is to be considered a true miracle, a Grade A miracle. God the Creator must intervene in one or both of these two universal laws, creating new matter or energy or organized complexity to accomplish His immediate purpose.

These two laws also testify to the existence of God. That is, everything is tending to decay and death and, indeed, the whole universe is heading inexorably toward complete disintegration. This is the testimony of the second law. The universe must somehow have started in the past, yet it could not have created itself; the first law assures us of that, since nothing is being created in a world governed by the present laws.

But it must have been created somehow, or else it would already be dead. Somehow, it was "wound up," so to speak, by something or someone outside of itself, capable of creating a mighty universe of infinite size, eternal duration, and a limitless variety of systems and processes, including life and soul and spirit.

"In the beginning God created"! That is the only logical conclusion to which one can come as based solely on the testimony of the two most basic and universal scientific laws governing all natural processes.

There is a wonderful verse in the Bible that beautifully anticipates these truths. That verse is Romans 1:20:

> *For the invisible things of him from the creation of the world are clearly seen, being understood by the things that are made, even his eternal power and Godhead, so that they are without excuse.*

Just how can invisible things be seen? The answer is that they can be *"understood by the things that are made,"* and they should have been seen *"from the creation of the world,"* being there ever since the beginning. And these things are so clearly *there* that those who don't see them are *"without excuse."*

As we have just noted, all these *"things that are made"* operate within a triune dimensional framework which is a perfect model of *"the Godhead,"* and their activities always function in accordance with the two universal laws whose only possible ultimate source was God's *"eternal power."* Thus *"even His eternal power and Godhead"* can be *"clearly seen, being understood"* by the *"the things that are made,"* and those who refuse to see are *"without excuse."*

Men try to *make* excuses, however, because the *"natural man receiveth not the things of the Spirit of God,"* and is actually spiritually *"dead in trespasses and sins"* and therefore does not even *want* to see God (1 Cor. 2:14; Eph. 2:1). The fact is that many of the antediluvians soon had *"changed the truth of God into a lie, and worshipped and served the creature more than the Creator"* (Rom. 1:25), and men have been believing the same lie (in various garbs, of course) ever since.

Nevertheless, the evidence is *there!* The unwillingness of men to look at the evidence was illustrated by an experience with the publishers of an engineering textbook I wrote many years ago. I had written a senior/graduate level textbook on hydraulic engineering for use in my classes at Virginia Tech and sent the manuscript to a number of possible publishers. Several leading science and engineering firms all wanted to publish it (McGraw-Hill, Macmillan, John Wiley, Van Nostrand, Ronald Press) and each offered me a contract. I signed on with Ronald Press, and they did publish it in 1962. Ronald eventually sold it to John Wiley, who then, in 1973, published it in an updated and enlarged edition. It has been used in at least 75 universities in this country and also quite widely in other countries, remaining in print even today.

However, they balked at including my exposition of Romans 1:20, showing how the laws of thermodynamics and dimensional analysis, which were both very useful in hydraulics, had been anticipated in the

Bible. I had always devoted part of one class lecture to this exposition in my classes in fluid mechanics, hydraulic engineering, and hydraulic models, since the laws of thermodynamics and dimensional analysis were fundamentally important in these subjects. No student ever objected and in fact usually this discussion was appreciated by the class, so I thought it appropriate to include it in the text I was writing.

But the publishers would not hear of it! They were well aware of the fracas back in 1950 when Macmillan published *Worlds in Collision*, by Immanuel Velikovsky, and the whole scientific community threatened to boycott all Macmillan's science books unless they took it out of publication. This was not a Christian book, of course (Velikovsky himself was an atheist), but its author did reject the scientific dogma of uniformitarianism and took the biblical accounts of catastrophism seriously, and the geologists and astronomers, as well as most other scientists, would not tolerate such "heresy."

I did argue with my publishers and they relented to the extent of allowing one footnote in my treatment of the laws of fluid mechanics. That footnote was as follows:

> The universality of the two laws of thermodynamics should be stressed. They have been substantiated empirically wherever it has been possible to test them, but have been widely accepted as foundational in science only since the work of Clausius, Kelvin, and others in the latter part of the nineteenth century. The reason for their universal scope cannot be determined by science but is clarified by theology. Thus the first law enunciates the constancy of

the totality of matter and energy in the universe, the reason being that the primeval processes of creation were terminated at the end of the six days of creation (see Gen. 2:1–3; Heb. 4:3–10). The second law in its broadest form states that there is a continual tendency toward disorder, decay, and death in the universe. This is best explained in terms of the curse pronounced by the Creator on the entire earth as a result of the introduction of moral rebellion in the world (see Gen. 1:31; 3:17–19; Rom. 8:20–22). The obvious conflict of these scientific laws with the previously popularized philosophy of universal evolutionary progress has not yet been adequately recognized (see *Applied Hydraulics in Engineering*, now published by John Wiley and Sons, New York, 1973, p. 26).

This "famous footnote," as it came to be widely called, attracted considerable interest, but never produced a call for boycott or demand for book removal, as Velikovsky's book did. I think that was because the users of the book were engineers, who usually are not nearly as committed to evolutionism as the "pure scientists" are. The book has remained in use for 40 years, which is very rare for an engineering book.

His Eternal Power and Godhead

But *this* book is supposed to be about miracles, not natural processes (maybe the long survival of this particular textbook could be considered a miracle of providence!). Anyway, the point of this particular discussion is to show that even the *natural* processes and laws of science give their own testimony to the reality of God and special creation. This is not just in a vague general science, either, but indicating *"His eternal power and Godhead."*

As far as power is concerned, power — technically speaking — is the time-rate of energy use in a system, where energy is equal to work, and work is the product of the force being exerted and the distance through which it works. Thus, work and energy are measured commonly in foot-pounds, and power is energy per second. For our purposes here, the terms "energy" and "power" are interchangeable. Thus, the first law says that, although power can change form (electrical power, kinetic power, etc.), the total power in a closed system is "conserved," remaining unchanged in quantity. Yet the "available power" for further work is decreasing, in accord with the second law.

Therefore, the source of the power (or energy) of the system cannot be "temporal power," since its useable power decreases with time. The power must have had a source somewhere, however; otherwise the system would already be dead, since it is "dying" in time. If it cannot be temporal power, the source must be eternal power. As Romans 1:20 says, God's *"eternal power"* is *"clearly seen"* in all the natural processes of the universe.

Similarly, the triune godhead is clearly seen in the space/time/matter structure of the universe. "Space," like the Father, is the background of all reality; "matter," like the Son, is the entity whereby the reality of space is seen; "time," like the Spirit, is that through which matter and space are experienced in actual working relationships. As noted before, the universe is "one" — not part space, part matter, part time. Each of the three pervades the whole — a universe, not a tri-verse. Likewise, God is not three Gods but one God: Father, Son, and Spirit are each totally God — one God.

Furthermore, each of the three entities in the universe is itself a tri-unity. Space is three-dimensional (length, width, and height), with each dimension occupying the whole of space. To get the quantity of space in a system, one does not add the three dimensions. Similarly, the "mathematics" of the Trinity is not 1 + 1 + 1 = 3, but 1 x 1 x 1 = 1. One God, yet three persons. Space is measured in terms of its first dimension (e.g., feet, square feet, cubic feet), but it can only be "seen" in the second dimension (as in two-dimensional photos, blueprints, book pages, etc.). But then we can only "experience" space in three dimensions.

Similarly, the time dimension is a trinity of future time, present time, and past time, with each comprising all the time that ever was, ever is, or ever will be. Just as space is identified in the first dimension, seen in the second, and experienced in the third, so time has its source in the unseen future, its manifestation in the present, becoming experienced time in the past. In both these sentences, one can substitute the words "Father," "Son," and "Spirit," and the same sentences will apply.

Matter (now known to be equivalent to energy) can be expressed in terms of the unseen energy source perpetually generating measurable activity whose motions can be actually measured, which then produce various phenomena. For example, unseen light energy generates light motion, which we experience in seeing the light. Sound energy produces sound waves which we experience in hearing the sound. Energy generates motion which we experience in phenomena. That is the tri-unity of matter.

The universe thus can be said to be a trinity of trinities. This is a remarkable phenomenon. Admittedly, it does not *prove* that God is a Trinity. However, there must be a Cause of such a remarkable effect. It would be eminently reasonable to conclude that a tri-universe was created as a testimony to the triune God who created it, and it is difficult to imagine any other cause that could explain it — certainly not random chance.

Thus, even the natural laws and processes of the universe — the very entities that scientists study — clearly reveal the infinite power of God and the triune nature of God. Scientists, of all people, are without excuse when they deny or ignore God.

For those desiring a fuller treatment of this intriguing subject, it is discussed in more detail in my book *The Biblical Basis for Modern Science* (chapters 2 and 3, pages 50–74), published in a new edition in 2002 by Master Books. So far as I know, the idea was first suggested many years ago by Nathan Wood, one-time president of Gordon College. Again, even without any miracles, the natural laws and processes of the cosmos testify to the reality of God — not only in their beauty and complexity, but also in their operations and very structure.

And the earth was without form, and void;

and darkness was upon the face of the

deep. And the Spirit of God moved upon

the face of the waters.

(Genesis 1:2)

NATURE IS THE ART

OF GOD ETERNAL.

— DANTE ALIGHIERI, 1265–1321

CHAPTER III

The Miracles of Primeval History

I n the previous chapter I discussed briefly the nature of natural laws and processes, noting that a real supernatural miracle would have to go against one or more of these laws. In particular the first and second laws of thermodynamics were defined and emphasized, since these two laws are known to govern all natural processes, with no exception yet found to either of them, *except* in miracles!

But where did *these laws* come from? What or who is the lawgiver who enacted these laws, and when were they enacted? They could not have just happened on their own. As noted before, the second law (indicating that everything tends to decay and go toward death) would assure us that the laws (and everything else) must have had a beginning in time, or else everything would already have decayed and died. But the first law (indicating that nothing is now being created) tells us that the universe, with all its systems and processes, could not have created itself.

The necessary conclusion is that the universe of space, matter, and time must have been created miraculously by a great Cause able to create a functioning universe. That Cause, by the principle of cause-and-effect (no effect greater than its cause), must have implicitly encompassed all the characteristics of that universe so created — characteristics including energy, matter, structure, life, personality, and morality. That Cause could be nothing less than the God of the Bible, for He alone could have been able to create the heavens and the earth, with all their features and all their inhabitants.

Furthermore, He did it in six solar days, and then "rested" on the seventh, providing a pattern for man to follow (Exod. 20:8–11). The processes of creation are no longer in operation, so they cannot be duplicated or studied today. They did not include any processes of death, so no fossils could have been formed during the creation period.

This mighty Creator not only operated against the first law of thermodynamics, but also *established* it, once the creation was finished. *"God saw every thing that He had made, and, behold, it was very good"* (Gen. 1:31). *"Thus the heavens and the earth were finished, and all the host of them"* (Gen. 2:1). He is now conserving what He created, *"upholding all things by the Word of His power"* (Heb. 1:3).

This primeval miracle of creation of all things is arguably not only the first miracle, but also the supreme miracle, with God simply speaking into existence everything that exists!

Many people, unfortunately, refuse to believe that it happened in the way God said it did, and try to explain the origin of the universe and its inhabitants by some naturalistic evolutionary growth process. In the living world, most biologists try to explain living creatures by a Darwinian process of variation and natural selection.

But all this is utterly futile! No one can cite a single example in all human history of such an evolution of a living thing ever happening. And certainly no one has ever seen a star evolve, or a galaxy, or anything else.

Variations are common, of course, but this is "horizontal" change, at the same level of complexity. "Vertical" changes into higher levels of organization and complexity never occur, as far as scientific observation is concerned. True evolution, therefore, is not happening at all in the present.

But what about the past? Anything can happen if enough time is available, they say, and evolutionists tend to believe in a *very* old cosmos — say 15 billion years for the universe, 4.6 billion years for the earth, about a billion or so years for life, and perhaps a million years for human life.

Now, billions of fossils have been entombed in the crust of the earth — mostly marine invertebrates, but also including abundant representatives of all the other phyla, as well as, in particular, most orders and families of vertebrates. Practically all — certainly most

— living families of animals can be found as fossils, including man. Evolutionists have tried to organize all these data into a sedimentary "column" for the geological material, and corresponding evolutionary "trees" of life for the biological. But these systems are arbitrary, largely based on the presupposition of evolution. And in spite of this evolutionary premise, these billions of organized fossils and sequences contain *no* transitional series from one kind (or family) into another more complex kind. A leading evolutionary anthropologist has commented on this uncomfortable fact as follows:

> Instead of filling in the gaps in the fossil record with so-called missing links, most paleontologists found themselves facing a situation in which there were only gaps in the fossil record, with no evidence of transformational intermediates between documented fossil species (Jeffrey H. Schwartz, *Sudden Origins*, John Wiley & Sons, 1999, p. 89).

Thus, with nothing but gaps in the fossil record, there is no real evidence that evolution ever occurred in the past, any more than in the present.

This absence of evidence is not surprising, because the second law of thermodynamics would indicate that true evolution, in the sense of growing complexity and organization, proceeding all the way from prokaryotes to human beings, could probably never happen at all. The second law, also known as the law of increasing entropy (or randomness), states the obvious fact that all *observed* processes tend to go in the direction of increasing *dis*organization (not the opposite, as evolution would suggest).

This fact raises the question as to the origin of this second law of thermodynamics. As we have noted above, the first law reflects the completion and subsequent maintenance of God's work of creation. But why would God plan to uphold the *quantity* of His creation, and not the *quality*? Why would He allow His "very good" creation to run down and disintegrate, in accord with the second law?

We need to remember that "why" questions can never be answered scientifically. Science can deal with "what," "how," "where," and sometimes "when," but never with "why." That type of question requires a philosophical answer — or, even better, theological.

The only real answer to the problem of decay and death in a "very good" creation is the entrance of *disorder* from outside. Increasing entropy, randomness, disintegration, decay, and other such terms are really just quasi-scientific ways of denoting sin, or spiritual rebellion and disorder coming into God's perfect creation.

God's creation had been placed under the caretaking stewardship of man, the highest of His creations, made in the very image of God. The tragedy was that, when the first man Adam was tested after being given freedom of choice, he failed the test, and sin came into the world. Not only man but also the entire creation that had been placed under his care had to come under God's "curse" for a time. *"Cursed is the ground for thy sake,"* God told Adam (Gen. 3:17), and ever since, *"We know that the whole creation groaneth and travailteth in pain together until now"* (Rom. 8:22).

This "curse" of God upon the whole creation (originally "very good" but now "groaning in pain") is the reason "why" the second law of thermodynamics applies to all natural processes, without exception. Two eminent physicists, E.H. Lieb and Jakob Yngvason, have recently reaffirmed this awesome truth, as noted in the previous chapter: "No exception to the second law of thermodynamics has ever been found — not even a tiny one" ("A Fresh Look at Entropy and the Second Law of Thermodynamics," *Physics Today*, vol. 53, April 2000, p. 32).

The imposition of the first law followed the completion of the good creation. Then the imposition of the second law accompanied the Curse. Both affected the whole creation and thus were both tremendous global miracles. As universal laws, established by God, they can be changed only by God. When either law is temporarily set aside for some specific divine purpose, God is required for its accomplishment, and I call such supernatural events miracles of creation, or "Grade A" miracles. "Grade B" miracles, on the other hand, need not require supernatural interference in one of the laws of thermodynamics, but rather a providential statistical ordering of some process or processes operating within the two laws in some very unusual way to meet a special need. Both of these will be discussed in more detail in subsequent chapters.

It is important to emphasize again that the supreme miracle of all miracles was the creation of the universe by God. There have been many attempts over the ages to explain the universe and its inhabitants by some process of evolution. That would be necessary, in fact, for Satan to rationalize his long war against God. However, all such evolutionary speculations have failed, and continue to fail, on the three essential points mentioned above. Evolution does not occur in the present, as all human history attests. Evolution clearly did not occur in the past; otherwise there should be many fossil vestiges of evolutionary transitions among the multitudes of fossils preserved in the rocks, but none are to be found anywhere. Most importantly, evolution cannot occur at all, because the second law of thermodynamics (actually God's curse on all the basic elements of matter) precludes it.

By evolution, of course, I am referring to macroevolution, the "vertical" evolution of one kind into a more complex kind. Microevolution, which has occurred frequently, is simply horizontal change at the same level of complexity. Nothing new is added, just simply a recombination of extant genes. The Bible requires only the conservation of "kinds," not varieties or even species or genera; the "kind" possibly in most cases is comparable to the taxonomist's "family," and there is no evidence whatsoever that the family line has ever been violated by any type of evolution.

There is one more great miracle of primeval history that affected the entire world — namely, the flood in the days of Noah. That flood was sent by God because of the global rebellion, wickedness, and violence that had developed since the creation and Curse. It was so devastating that the Lord Jesus said, some 2,500 years or more later, that *"The flood came, and destroyed them all"* (Luke 17:27), and the apostle Peter said that *"The world that then was, being overflowed with water, perished"* (2 Pet. 3:6).

The Greek word translated "overflowed" in the latter verse is the word from which we transliterate our English word "cataclysm," and always in the New Testament was applied only to that flood in the days of Noah. The Flood was not only a flood of waters that covered all the mountains but also was accompanied by great tectonic and volcanic upheavals, tremendous erosion and deposition of sediments, the wholesale destruction and burial of all forms of plant and animal life, followed by strong winds and extensive glaciation, as well as the destruction of all human life except those people on Noah's ark.

The initial cause of the great cataclysm is recorded as twofold: (1) *". . . the same day were all the fountains of the great deep broken up,"* and (2) *"the windows of heaven were opened. And the rain was upon the earth forty days and forty nights"* (Gen. 7:11–12). Whether these were caused directly by God or whether there were secondary causes that God used to produce these catastrophic activities is not stated and so comprises a legitimate question for research. In any case, the most important result was that *"every living substance was destroyed which was upon the face of the ground, both man, and cattle, and the creeping things, and the fowl of the heaven; and they were destroyed from the earth: and Noah only remained alive, and they that were with him on the ark"* (Gen. 7:23).

In view of the tremendous power of moving water and volcanic eruptions, there can be no doubt that vast numbers of living creatures were entombed in the rushing sediments, eventually becoming fossilized. This fossil record, all over the world, and the lithified or compacted sediments that entombed them, have long been called the "geologic column," and have been commonly misinterpreted by evolutionists as giving a summary record of earth's long evolutionary history. The straightforward biblical record, however, would indicate that the geologic column is *not* the record of the evolutionary development of life over many ages, but rather of the worldwide extinction of life in one great cataclysm centered mainly in the days of Noah.

Modern geologists, while still adhering to the standard evolutionary framework, are becoming more and more convinced that each individual formation in the earth's crust was formed rapidly, even catastrophically. This "new catastrophism," as it has been called, is rapidly displacing the old-style "uniformitarianism" which had been favored since the days of Hutton and Lyell in the early 19th century. One of the leaders among these modern geologists is Derek Ager, who wrote entire books showing that everything in the geologic column had been produced very rapidly. The final sentence of one key book said that "the history of any one part of the earth . . . consists of long periods of boredom and short periods of terror" (*The Nature of the Stratigraphical Record*, John Wiley & Sons Publishers, 2nd Edition, 1993, p. 141).

Dr. Ager took great pains to assure readers he still accepted the long ages of the standard system and did not believe in the Bible or the God of the Bible. Nevertheless, he rejected what he called "the dangerous doctrine of uniformitarianism" and insisted that "in all branches of geology there has been a return to ideas of rare violent happenings and episodicity" (*The New Catastrophism*, Cambridge University Press, 1993, p. xvi, xii). Dr. Warren Allmon, reviewing the latter book, stressed that "the geological record is dominated not by slow, gradual change but by episodic rare events causing local disasters." He hailed the work of Ager and others as marking "the arrival of catastrophism at the status quo" ("Post-Gradualism," *Science*, vol. 262, Oct. 1, 1993, p. 122).

Now, if every unit of the geologic column was formed rapidly and that is what these up-to-date geologists are saying, where are the postulated millions and billions of years? Could they be in the gaps between formations, the "periods of boredom" cited by Ager?

No, because there is no worldwide gap, and therefore no missing time period or periods in the entire geologic column. The column was formed continuously by sedimentation (always proceeding rapidly) with local gaps (that is, periods of erosion) at different places at different times, yet no worldwide time gap! The only exception is at the very bottom of the geologic column, where the sediments of the column all rest upon the crystalline rocks at the so-called "basement." No geologist would dispute this statement.

The whole is the sum of its parts. If all components of the geologic column were produced catastrophically and rapidly, and no worldwide gap exists between these components, the necessary conclusion is that the entire column was formed rapidly and continuously — in one great sequence of catastrophes that combined to produce a great cataclysm, in which *"the world that then was, being overflowed* [that is, 'cataclysmed'] *with water, perished"* (2 Pet. 3:6).

So the third primeval global miracle was the Flood (or, better, the cataclysm), which marks a sharp boundary between the antediluvian world and this present world system. Significantly, so far as is known, the cataclysm did not involve a supernatural suspension of either of the laws of thermodynamics, so it was not a "Grade A" miracle! However, it was certainly the most extensive and profound "Grade B" miracle that ever occurred, with so many natural processes exorbitantly accelerated and intensified (precipitation, erosion, tectonism, etc.) to a degree never experienced before or since.

The creation was the greatest "Grade A" miracle of all time, the cataclysm the greatest "Grade B" miracle. The Curse is difficult to define in either category, although to overcome it in any specific instance would, indeed, require a "Grade A" miracle. It is significant that the time is coming where there shall be "no more curse" (Rev. 22:3).

Creation, curse, cataclysm. These were the three great miracles of the primeval age. The full recognition of all three of these is essential to the development of a valid world view. The latter has been called, mainly by its opponents, "young-earth creationism," but I believe it is simply *the biblical world view*.

Other world views, whether they are called "theistic evolution," "progressive creation," "old-earth creation," or some variant thereof — not to mention "atheistic evolutionism" — all are really libels on the character of a holy, loving, merciful Creator God. That is, they all profess billions of years of a groaning creation (including death) prior to the entrance of sin into the world and the subsequent imposition of God's curse thereon. Thus, they implicitly charge God with pointless blundering and sadistic cruelty in His supposed eons-long work of "creation," as well as what seems a pitiful charade in requiring the death of His Son to atone for human sin when death was presumably an important "agent" in the evolution of human life in the first place.

They should not do that!

And the locusts went up over all the land
of Egypt, and rested in all the coasts of
Egypt: very grievous were they; before
them there were no such locusts as they,
neither after them shall be such.

(Exodus 10:14)

SCIENCE HAS SOMETIMES BEEN SAID TO BE OPPOSED
TO FAITH AND INCONSISTENT WITH IT. BUT ALL
SCIENCE, IN FACT, RESTS ON A BASIS OF FAITH, FOR
IT ASSUMES THE PERMANENCE AND UNIFORMITY OF
NATURAL LAWS — A THING WHICH CAN NEVER BE
DEMONSTRATED.

— TRYON EDWARDS, 1809–1894

CHAPTER IV

Miracles Versus the Laws of Science

As mentioned in chapter I, it has long been contended by scientists that true miracles are impossible. Everything that happens, they say, can really be explained, at least in principle, by the ordinary processes of nature. There is surely need for more research, they willingly agree, but any happenings that seem at first to be inexplicable scientifically are potentially capable of a naturalistic explanation, they are sure, and it is impossible to prove

otherwise. The tendency to attribute some unusual event to a miracle is simply a resort to the old "God-of-the-gaps" copout, and this strategy (or lack thereof) is universally derided by scientists.

The Scientific Impossibility of Miracles

All throughout history, and especially since the time of David Hume (1711–1776), skeptical philosophers have insisted that it is impossible to prove a miracle. There are always several possibilities for explaining away any alleged miracle, they have argued.

For one thing, the testimony of its witnesses may be mistaken, sometimes even fraudulent. But even when the witnesses are perfectly sincere in their reports, honestly believing that a miracle has indeed occurred, one can never really be sure. Our senses often deceive us, especially in situations highly charged emotionally, such as in the presence of what seems to be something miraculous. For that matter, in any exciting circumstance, such as an automobile accident, say, it is often hard to find two or more witnesses who will agree on exactly how it happened.

Even if the witnesses cannot be impugned and can accurately describe the unusual event, that still does not prove it was a miracle. It may be a phenomenon that is perfectly natural, but one which does not yet have a satisfactory scientific explanation. Further study and research may well yield a completely naturalistic accounting of it.

Back in the time of David Hume, if someone had been able to travel from London to New York in five hours, even he might have called it a miracle. Now we just call it an airplane! If people in Los Angeles just a hundred years ago could have watched a baseball game being played in Philadelphia, they surely would have called it a miracle. Now it's called television.

These so-called "miracles of modern science and technology" are almost innumerable today, but they have resulted from intensive research and development and are now considered commonplace. They are not supernatural at all. There still exist strange phenomena we don't yet understand, but that doesn't mean they are miraculous. Further scientific research may well yield a purely natural explanation. Or at least we cannot be sure it will not, the scientists would say.

This would be particularly likely if the phenomenon occurs often and thereby satisfies the scientific principle of repeatability. A somewhat controversial example might be what some believe to be a supernatural "gift of tongues" — the ability under some circumstances to speak in some other tongue, either a foreign language or some "unknown tongue." Many so-called charismatic Christians profess to have this gift but, since it is reproducible, often at will, it really seems to be a natural process which is not yet completely understood, but probably does have a psychological or physiological explanation needing further research. The ability to speak like this in a sort of ecstatic gibberish is frequently encountered in other religions as well as among some Christian groups. In the absence of further research, it is hard to *prove* that this phenomenon is not really a natural process (some might say demonic, but that's another question) which has not *yet* been adequately studied scientifically.

But if the witnesses of the alleged miracle turn out to be completely reliable, and the event is so unique that it seems absolutely impossible to describe scientifically, there is still another possible way to avoid calling it a miracle. That is, it may turn out to be merely an extreme statistical variation of a natural process. For example, a very heavy rain, vastly exceeding all previous rainfall records, might suddenly occur in a region, and people might call it a miracle, especially if they had been praying for rain after a long drought. And perhaps it could be considered a sort of providential miracle, even if it resulted just from a rare combination of the physical phenomena that produce rain, rather than something supernatural.

Other devices might also be used to "explain" the alleged miracle, but in any case most scientists would insist that true supernatural miracles are impossible. Either the witnesses were mistaken, the event was natural even though not yet completely explained scientifically, it was merely a statistical oddity, or some other device could be suggested, so that the phenomenon was not *really* a miracle after all.

But Miracles Do Happen

And still the Bible records many *real miracles*, which no such device has ever yet been able to explain away. One thinks of the miracles attributed to Moses and Joshua, to Elijah and Elisha, and various others, especially those performed by the Lord Jesus Christ.

When Nicodemus, one of the greatest teachers in Israel, went to see Jesus one night, he acknowledged that Jesus must have come from God, for, said he, *"No man can do these miracles that thou doest, except God be with him"* (John 3:2). During Christ's ministry on earth, He performed many miracles, especially miraculous healings, all of them with some immediate human need in mind and never just for show, yet also to demonstrate that He was indeed the Son of God.

Before going much further, however, we still need to define exactly what we mean by miracles. It is obvious that, to say miracles are impossible is the same as saying that there is no God — and that is utter folly (note Ps. 14:1 — *"The fool hath said in his heart, There is no God"*). It obviously is impossible to prove that there is no God! Even the atheistic biochemist Isaac Asimov, probably the most prolific science writer of all time, acknowledged that he could not prove there was no God. If God conceivably could have created the world and ordained its laws, then He certainly can set them aside, or supersede them, if He so wills. Thus, it is impossible to *prove* that miracles are impossible.

Yet, admittedly, miracles are so rare that scientists and others can make a somewhat persuasive case, as we have seen, that they never occur at all, and that any alleged miracle can be explained naturalistically if examined closely enough.

So we can begin our attempt at a definition by admitting that miracles are scientifically impossible, but insisting that they do (or at least did) happen anyway, thus "breaking" one or more scientific laws. That brings us back to having to recognize the laws that miracles break when they do happen.

That is not as hard to do as some might have assumed. We have noted in the previous chapter that there are really just two universal laws of science, and that all real processes — physical, chemical, biological, etc. — always operate within the constraints of these two laws, the first and second laws of thermodynamics. Thus, a miracle can be tentatively defined as an event that "disobeys" one or both of these laws.

The first law of thermodynamics is the law of conservation of energy (with the understanding that energy includes not only electrical, heat, sound, light energy, etc., but also even matter itself). It states that energy can be changed in form — from electricity to light, for example — but not in total quantity. The "state" of matter can be changed — from solid to liquid, for example — but not its total mass, with one exception. Mass and energy can be exchanged under certain very special conditions. That is, mass can be converted into energy, in nuclear fission processes, and energy into matter, in thermo-nuclear fusion processes. When these occur, the totality of mass and energy is conserved, as expressed in the famous Einstein equation, $E = mc^2$, where c is the velocity of light, relating the mass m to its implicit energy E.

Thus, the first law of thermodynamics expresses the universally observed fact that the totality of mass and energy is always conserved, even though energy can change in form and matter in state. No exception to this law has ever been found (although certain current speculations are suggesting that may not always have been the case in the distant past). It is fair to say that this first law, or law of conservation of mass/energy, is the best-proved law of science.

The second law is also universally found to be true, with no valid exception ever observed. Although no known process involves either creation or annihilation of mass/energy, every known process involves a deterioration of mass/energy. That is, it somehow becomes less available for further useful "work."

For example, chemical energy stored in the gasoline can be converted to mechanical energy on the moving wheels of the automobile, but some is always converted into heat energy through friction of the wheels with the road surface. That heat energy is not annihilated, warming the space around the wheel a bit, but it can no longer be captured and converted into useful work.

This phenomenon is always encountered in every process. Some of the available energy for doing the needed work always has to be diverted through friction into heat energy, which is still "there" but no longer "available." This type of thing goes on everywhere in the universe, so the total mass/energy of the universe is also gradually being converted into low levels of useless heat energy, and the universe seems destined eventually to die a so-called "heat death," with uniform temperature everywhere and nothing happening anywhere — if, that is, these processes continue long enough without miraculous intervention.

Miracles of Creation (Grade A Miracles)

And that's the point! It would take a miracle to intervene in either of these two universal laws, and that's how we can define a real supernatural miracle. That is, a sudden creation of matter (as when Christ multiplied the loaves and fishes to feed the multitude — see Matt. 14:14–21) or creation of energy (as when the waters of the Red Sea were suspended by some kind of anti-gravitational energy as vertical walls to allow the Children of Israel to pass through the sea on a dry sea-bed and then allowed to collapse and drown Pharaoh's army when they tried to follow — see Exodus 14:21–28) — these would certainly be true miracles, incapable of any naturalistic explanation except by flat denial that the records as we have them are true.

These would be properly recognized as miracles of creation. I call them "Grade A miracles." Such miracles are extremely rare today, if

they happen at all, and would require absolutely iron-clad historical and testimonial evidence of verification before we should accept
them as real. With one exception, that is. The miracle of regeneration is called a *"new creation"* (2 Cor. 5:17) and it does, indeed, often
occur even today. This type of miracle is discussed further in chapter
VII.

Other types of Grade A miracles are bound to be very rare. The
"laws" of nature, especially the two universal laws of thermodynamics, have been established by God for good reasons. Although God
certainly can supersede them if He so wills, there needs to be sufficient reason for Him to do so, as well as irrefutable evidence that
He has. The stories of such miracles of creation more often than not
seem to flounder on these two requirements.

A miracle that would go against the first law means there would
have to be an actual *creation* or absolute *annihilation* of mass or energy. A miracle against the second law would mean creation of a
higher order of organized complexity, or information, in a given system — in every case without a natural source of the matter or energy
or complexity or information available to that system.

Such instances are obviously extremely rare, though possible.
One missionary lady told me, for example, of an event much like
the miraculously replenished barrel of meal and cruse of oil belong-
ing to a widow woman in Zarephath in the days of Elijah (1 Kings
17:8–16). This godly lady, also a widow with one son, had been
serving as a missionary in China with her husband until his death.
This was during the time when the Chinese Communists were
seeking to take over the land of China and were invading many
of its rural provinces. A band of Communists had laid siege to the

missionary compound where she was, and the rice supply was all the food they had left. However, that supply somehow seemed to maintain its same low level, despite daily withdrawals for meals, for many days. Finally the invaders left without ever entering the missionary compound. The rice, she said, seemed to miraculously replenish itself all that time.

The only evidence I had of this Grade A miracle, of course, was her testimony, and this was probably not enough to be sure that this was, indeed, a miracle of creation.

However, she was certainly a very godly woman, who had served faithfully in China for many years, and surely would not intentionally lie about such a matter. I believe it really happened, but only because I have confidence in her testimony. It would be understandable if others may not agree.

What about miraculous healings? No doubt, many of these are psychosomatic in nature. The body's innate powers to heal itself are very substantial, particularly when somehow encouraged by psychological or mental factors. Also, some healings that have been considered miraculous are most likely related to slowing down the decay processes associated with the particular disease or condition, rather than the actual creation of new information or organization in the ailing member of the body.

Yet some do seem to involve more than that sort of thing. The most obvious such "healing" would be an actual restoration of physical life in one who had died — such as Lazarus or Dorcas or others cited in the Bible. There have indeed been a number of such resuscitations reported in recent years, as doctors have managed by certain procedures to revive people who had been first pronounced dead. Many of these folks have even reported certain "after-death experiences" while they were presumably physically lifeless. These are too many of these to call them hoaxes or hallucinations or any such thing.

My own mother (Mrs. Ida Morris) went through one of these over 50 years ago while visiting us in Minneapolis, during the time I was teaching and doing graduate work at the University of Minnesota. She had experienced heart trouble from time to time most of her adult life. But while visiting us, she had a serious attack and was sent to the Lutheran Deaconess Hospital there in Minneapolis and seemed to be recovering. Then one late morning I received an emergency call in my office, telling me to rush to the hospital. My mother had had a coronary thrombosis there in the hospital and was apparently dying.

It was a long drive from the university to the hospital, and I hurried there as fast as I could. However, about halfway there, I was stopped in traffic by what seemed an interminable freight train. I was praying earnestly all the way, especially while stopped for the train, asking God to please keep her alive until I could get there at least to pray with her and say goodbye.

When I finally arrived, I was greeted excitedly by the doctors and nurses, all of whom were Christians, saying they had seen a miracle! My mother had actually died and all hope had been given up after every attempt to revive her had failed.

But then, suddenly, she opened her eyes and began excitedly telling everyone she had seen how beautiful heaven was, and had even seen my younger brother John, who had been killed in World War II not too long before. She heard beautiful music (she herself was a gifted pianist) and saw beautiful lights. But then she was apparently called back to the hospital room, where she saw the doctors and nurses around her apparently lifeless body in the bed.

Whether this was a true miracle, I don't know, but the doctors and nurses were all convinced it was. So was I, feeling it was an answer to my prayers while stalled there at the railroad crossing.

Mother was always happy to tell about her experience, and she never had any heart trouble after that. However, several years later, in her apartment back in Houston, she had severe chest pains one day and went to the hospital, fearing it might be another heart attack. It turned out, rather, to be her gall bladder, which the doctors therefore removed and she was okay.

The remarkable thing about this was that, in the process, they examined her heart, and reported back that the heart showed no signs at all of ever having been damaged! It does seem that the Lord somehow had made her dying heart whole again! Although I have read a number of reports of somewhat similar (but not quite) "near-death experiences" in the 55 or so years since, Mother's was the first I ever heard of, and it still seems different from these later ones. I like to think it may really have been a modern Grade A type of miracle.

We do know that our Lord Jesus Christ in His days here on earth, healed many who were dying, and even brought three people who were truly dead back to life again, and He is *"the same yesterday, and to day, and for ever"* (Heb. 13:8). Grade A miracles, requiring His power as Creator, are surely very rare today (except for the miracle of the new birth), but they can happen when He so wills.

We can also discuss Grade B miracles, which occur today with much greater frequency — that is, miracles which don't require

interfering in the two universal laws of thermodynamics. That will be the subject of the next chapter.

The Miraculous Nature of Evolution

Before closing this chapter, however, it is appropriate to refer to the bizarre pseudo-scientific idea of evolution. Evolution allegedly embraces the origin and development of everything, purporting to explain how nothing evolved into the primeval universe, how a primeval particle of space/time evolved into hydrogen, then hydrogen into all the other elements, how the elements evolved into stars and planets, how the elements on one planet in particular evolved into living organisms, how the first protozoa evolved into metazoa, then how the first vertebrates evolved from invertebrates, how fishes evolved into amphibians, then into reptiles, birds, mammals, and people.

Note that this array would have required one Grade A miracle after another — first the creation of matter itself, in violation of the first law, then a creation of new information and organization, in violation of the second law, at every step along the way. What a paradox! Evolution is supposed to be the scientific explanation of origins — replacing the old naïve idea of special creation — but it does so by postulating an almost infinite series of miracles of creation in order to get from primeval particles (and even these have to come out of nothing!) to planets and people. Evolution may be a very influential man-pleasing philosophy, since it allegedly makes the idea of God and creation redundant, but it does so by assuming an infinite array of imaginary creations to replace the one creation by the omnipotent Creator God. It professes to be scientific, but it breaks the basic laws of science over and over and over again. It is truly a remarkable concept.

A recent development has been, if possible, even more bizarre. A number of evolutionary scientists have developed a new "science" which they call "chaos theory," including the notion that order can arise out of chaos. The theory is largely mathematical, rather than experimental, but it does have value in its analysis of chaotic systems themselves, especially as they have "devolved" from previously ordered systems. However, to hope that the process can somehow reverse itself and generate order out of chaos is wishful thinking at best.

It is significant that the examples they can cite of orderly systems arising in a chaotic environment are called "dissipative structures," because their structured order is achieved at the cost of even greater dissipation of energy in the surroundings. The most common examples used are the generation of vortices in a coffee cup and the generation of tornadoes in the atmosphere.

These may show a sort of "order," all right, but the result in the respective environments around these "structures" is an abnormally high dissipation of energy or organization. Despite any superficial exception to the second law, such dissipative structures actually demonstrate its validity, and certainly do not prove "evolution."

My God hath sent his angel, and hath shut the lions' mouths, that they have not hurt me: forasmuch as before him innocency was found in me; and also before thee, O king, have I done no hurt.

(Daniel 6:22)

MILLIONS OF SPIRITUAL CREATURES

WALK THE EARTH

UNSEEN, BOTH WHEN WE WAKE,

AND WHEN WE SLEEP:

ALL THESE WITH CEASELESS PRAISE

HIS WORKS BEHOLD

BOTH DAY AND NIGHT.

— JOHN MILTON, 1608–1674

CHAPTER V

Grade B Miracles and the Ministry of Angels

I have been calling miracles of creation — that is, miracles requiring intervention in one or both of the universal laws of science, the first and second laws of thermodynamics — "Grade A" miracles, requiring the creative powers of God himself to accomplish. Neither man nor angel can *create* something out of nothing (whether that something is energy or matter or a higher degree of organized complexity), so this type of miracle requires the power of either God himself or a special divinely energized representative of God (e.g., Paul the Apostle). Only the triune God is *the* Creator, as well as Redeemer and eternal King.

Miracles of Providence (Grade B Miracles)

However, there is no doubt that many remarkable events have occurred which could rightly be called miracles, even though they happened within the constraints of the two laws. These, I have called "Grade B" miracles or, more technically, miracles of providence. They involve no suspension of basic laws but rather some change in the functioning of a natural process operating within the laws — that is, a change of rate, or timing, or some other aspect of the process or processes producing the event in question.

An obvious example would be the earthquake that opened the doors of the prison in Philippi where Paul and Silas were singing hymns at midnight (Acts 16:25–27). Earthquakes are fairly common phenomena, but the *rate* of occurrence of earthquakes that open jails at Philippi at midnight when prisoners are praying and singing praises to God is very, very low! The same would be true of the 3½ years of drought in the land of Israel following the prayer of a prophet (James 5:17–18).

There are numerous examples of such Grade B miracles recorded in the Bible, more than the number of Grade A miracles, as noted further in chapter VII. It is interesting that, in many of these providential miracles, the Bible indicates that angels were involved. For example, it was an angel who caused the doors of the prison in Jerusalem, where the high priest had imprisoned the apostles, to open and free the prisoners (Acts 5:17–19).

The Role of Angels

God does have *"an innumerable company of angels"* (Heb. 12:22) ready to carry out His assignments. They *"excel in strength, that do His commandments, hearkening unto the voice of His word"* (Ps. 103:20). And one of His main angelic assignments is for them to serve as *"ministering spirits, sent forth to minister for them who shall be heirs of salvation"* (Heb. 1:14). That surely seems to mean that angels have been assigned to minister to those who have believed on Christ, presumably to meet some special need, and perhaps in answer to prayer.

Some angels, it would seem, have been assigned as guardian angels to little children (Matt. 18:10), and possibly to adult Christians as well. Some seem to have an ongoing ministry (unrealized but nonetheless real) to local churches (Rev. 1:20). All are said to *"desire to look into"* the workings of God toward our salvation (1 Pet. 1:12) and are somehow being shown *"by the church the manifold wisdom of God"* (Eph. 3:10).

It is thus reasonable to believe that God's angels are still active in these and other such ministries. And there is an abundance of testimonial evidence that this is indeed the case. Even though I have never, to my knowledge at least, either seen an angel personally or heard one speak, I do believe they are somehow near us and, indeed, ministering to us who are the present-day heirs of salvation. They are normally invisible to human eyes, being spirits, but do have the ability when necessary to assume physical bodies as men. The two angels who visited Lot in Sodom (Gen. 19:1–3) provide a vivid example. They looked like men, spoke like men, and even ate like men. But they were powerful enough to smite the invading Sodomites with blindness and then, by God's power and will, to destroy their wicked cities with *"fire from the LORD out of heaven"* (Gen. 19:11, 13, 24).

Angels have great wisdom (2 Sam. 14:20) as well as great strength (Ps. 103:20), though only God is omniscient and omnipotent. Although only God is omnipresent, the host of angels is so large in number that God can dispatch them throughout the whole world as needed, when we pray in accordance with His will.

Our oldest daughter, Kathleen, has been serving as a missionary linguist and counselor for well over 30 years with the Wycliffe Bible Translators, and is now teaching in their Graduate School of Applied Linguistics. She has been very spiritually minded and biblically knowledgeable from her earliest days, baptized at her insistence after thorough questioning by the pastor and deacons when she was only five years old, so small that she could not stand in the baptismal tank and had to be held in the pastor's arms as she went beneath the waters.

But she was also very high-spirited and adventuresome. I think she was about eight when she decided to ride her older brother's new bicycle. She had never ridden a bike before, but nevertheless thought she could do it. She got it out of the garage and, sure enough, she found she could get on and ride it out the driveway. But then she saw a car coming rapidly down the street and realized she did not know how to stop it.

The woman driving the car told me later that when she saw the bike heading into the street, she immediately tried to stop. In her panic, however, she mashed on the accelerator instead of the brake, and hit the bicycle full force, demolishing it. When I heard the crash, I ran out of the house to find little Kathy lying in the ditch by the side of the road, with the broken bike some distance away.

Naturally I was afraid my little daughter would be seriously injured or dead but, when I picked her up, she was all right. Other than being somewhat shaken, she was not injured at all.

Then, after I took her into the house, she told us what had happened. When she saw the car coming and suddenly realized she could not stop, she heard a voice telling her to take her feet off the pedals and lift them away. She obeyed the voice and, when the car struck the bicycle, she was simply thrown off and onto the grassy ditch while the riderless bike was being mangled under the car.

Well, I don't know. But in such a circumstance one could hardly avoid thinking of such a verse as Psalm 91:11–12, which says that *"He shall give His angels charge over thee, to keep thee in all thy ways. They shall bear thee up in their hands, lest thou dash thy foot against a stone."* The venerable old tradition of guardian angels is not just wishful thinking or pious imagery. It is a biblical doctrine.

Then there was the time when my son John sensed the presence of angels on Mount Ararat. John is our second son and is now president of the Institute for Creation Research, having taken over this responsibility in 1996 when I resigned from the position (I had founded the ICR in 1970 and stepped down 25 years later, at age 77).

Anyway, John had heard the unconfirmed stories of various sightings of Noah's ark high on Mount Ararat in eastern Turkey, and felt the Lord was leading him to find it and use its testimony as a witness for Christ in these latter days. He organized a team of four others to accompany him, raised the funds (mostly his own savings), arranged for mountain training, studied the Turkish language, got the necessary Turkish visas and permits, and set out for Turkey and Mount Ararat in the late summer of 1972.

After overcoming and surviving many dangers and difficulties, they finally got to the mountain and started to climb. All of this is described in a fascinating little book written by John based on his daily journal of the entire trip (*Adventure on Ararat*), published by ICR in 1973, but now out of print.

At the 14,000-foot level, they suddenly were enveloped in a violent snow storm which soon turned into an even more severe lightning storm. Then three of them, including John, were actually struck by a bolt of lightning. In his book, John described his own experience as follows:

> As all three of us stood or sat on this big rock, lightning struck it again, sending unbelievable jolts of electricity through us. J.B. . . . could see Roger and me thrown off the rock. The force of the lightning seemed to suspend us in the air and then dropped us far down the slope. . . . I expected an impact but it never came; it seemed like I was floating very slowly for several seconds. I was gently lain on the snow by unseen hands and began sliding down the steep slope" (*Adventure on Ararat*, p. 60–61).

This was only one of the almost lethal perils encountered on the mountain, but this was the one in which it seemed most directly that there must have been guardian angels involved, whose "unseen hands" carried them through the air and laid them gently on the slope. John did not actually *see* angels, but he was somehow sure of their presence.

As an interesting footnote, he recalled later how he had been quite rebellious as a teenager, even though he had accepted Christ when quite young and been baptized when he was nine. He occasionally would tell me during high school and college days that he knew he would serve the Lord some day, but that it would take a bolt of lightning to get him started! In any case, God preserved his life during that eventful trip to Mount Ararat (and several others that followed) and he has been faithfully and fruitfully serving the Lord ever since. We both believe that his lightning experience was a Grade B miracle and that angels were involved.

A more graphic experience of angelic protection was related to the college Sunday school class I was teaching in Minnesota some 50 or more years ago. Mrs. Vatsaas, a returned missionary from China, whose son Chris Vatsaas was in the class, was the same missionary that had told about the continually replenished supply of rice during the Communist siege of their compound in China a few years before. Her story was confirmed by Chris, who had been a young boy at the time.

According to her account, the climax of the siege came one night when the missionaries were expecting an imminent attack that would breach the walls of the compound and enable the Communists to kill the missionaries inside. Suddenly and inexplicably, however, the invaders seemed to change their minds and hasten away from the village altogether.

A year or so later, a converted Communist explained why. As they were about to attack and scale the wall, there appeared a great army of large fighting men on top of the entire wall surrounding the compound. This sight so frightened the Communist guerrillas that they immediately fled in terror.

The similarity of this deliverance to the time when Elisha's servant had his eyes opened to see the vast host of *"horses and chariots of fire"* protecting Elisha from the Syrian army (2 Kings 6:15–17) is evident. Similar stories have been related by a number of other missionaries serving in dangerous places. *"The angel of the LORD encampeth round about them that fear Him, and delivereth them"* (Ps. 34:7).

Several years ago, one of our ICR scientists, Dick Bliss, died of a sudden heart attack while in Iowa on a speaking assignment, leaving his lovely wife, Lolly, a widow living alone (their children were grown, married, and living in other states).

Lolly told how, soon afterwards, her car stalled on a busy freeway, at a point where the freeway was diverging into two freeways. She was stranded in the midst of those two diverging freeways and could do nothing except pray.

Suddenly a passing car stopped beside her, and a young man got out and in the midst of the traffic was able to get her car running again. He then immediately drove off without even giving her his name or any other information about himself. Was he an angel? Could be!

But not all Grade B miracles have to involve angels. Another fascinating account of such a miracle was related to my wife and me back about 1945, during the time I was teaching servicemen at Rice Institute (now known as Rice University). I had managed, by God's grace in answer to prayer, to start a campus Bible class, and we had seen much evidence of His blessing. Many students were being brought to Christ and saved there in a very secular university.

We decided to affiliate with the Inter-Varsity Christian Fellowship, in fact becoming one of the earliest IVCF groups in the United States (the Fellowship had begun some years previously in England and Canada).

One of our visiting IVCF speakers was a single lady named Irene Webster-Smith, who roomed with Mary Louise and me while she was ministering to our student Christian fellowship group, and she told us her story. She had served many years in Japan as headmistress of a school for Japanese orphan girls, and had led most of them to Christ. She had to leave Japan when our country went to war against Japan after the bombing of Pearl Harbor and had come on the staff of Inter-Varsity as a sort of roving missionary and Bible teacher.

The incident she told us about had to do with the orphan girls in her school. Their school was near the ocean, but they could not see the ocean because of an intervening hill that blocked the view. One day, when Miss Webster-Smith returned home after a trip of several days, they excitedly told her how God had answered their prayers and now they had a beautiful view of their beloved seashore.

They recalled how their teacher had read the teachings of Jesus to them, one of which even involved moving mountains. *"If ye have faith as a grain of mustard seed,"* Jesus had said, *"ye shall say unto this mountain, Remove hence to yonder place; and it shall remove; and nothing shall be impossible unto you"* (Matt. 17:20).

So, they reasoned, if believing prayer can move mountains, it ought to be able to move a small hill, and they undertook to pray for the removal of the hill. And, lo and behold, a construction crew in need of the material in the hill for some kind of building or roadway, did indeed come along shortly, and proceed to cut down the hill, just as the girls had prayed! Now they could see the ocean! I would call this a Grade B miracle, and a beautiful answer to prayer.

Undoubtedly, many readers of these lines could relate similar answers to prayer, some even involving angels. Grade A miracles may be very rare today (except for the miracle of the new birth, of course), but Grade B miracles do happen on occasion, usually in answer to fervent prayer, like that of Elijah (James 5:16–17).

Every believing and practicing Christian knows that God does answer prayer, often in very remarkable ways and circumstances — circumstances that skeptics might call odd coincidences (but we know better!). As noted previously, there is *"an innumerable company of angels"* whose chief purpose is to serve as *"ministering spirits, sent forth to minister for them who shall be heirs of salvation"* (Heb. 12:22; 1:14). Even though I have not yet seen those who have ministered to me and my family, I am confident they are there and have occasionally sensed their presence. I am looking forward to *really* meeting them in heaven, and thanking them for what they have done.

Miracles and Divine Watchcare

I guess that most of our prayers are sort of routine and general ("please bless my loved ones"), and perhaps the ministry of the angels God has assigned to us is also routine and general, but even this is invaluable. But when a special need arises, and we are moved to pray urgently and fervently, if God (perhaps using the angels) does answer and meet that need, *that's* when we are specially aware of His presence and power and when we then offer fervent prayers of special thanksgiving. And if the answer requires some very unusual timing or rate of otherwise natural processes, it might well be a miracle of providence, or Grade B miracle.

In one sense, of course, even God's routine watchcare could be considered miraculous in the providential sense. My wife, Mary Louise, and I have been married 64 years and have lived in 15 different homes in eight different cities in six different states. Each day we have prayed for God's protection and watchcare, and He has graciously answered that prayer in the sense that we have never been robbed nor our home damaged in a storm of any kind. At least we consider that an answer to prayer.

We prayed for God's guidance, of course, and we are confident that He has led in each of these various moves, with blessings resulting in abundance. All six of our children accepted Christ early in their lives, and are faithful witnessing Christians today (one, of course, already in heaven). All have at least two college degrees, and four have earned doctorates. They married Christian spouses and are earnestly trying to bring up our 17 grandchildren *"in the nurture and admonition of the Lord"* (Eph. 6:4). When people ask me how to raise godly children in such an ungodly age, I simply have to reply, "You pray a lot!"

This is not meant to be a book of testimony, however, so I'd better forego too many more personal illustrations of prayer answered. But the Bible is replete with promises of answered prayer, and they have been wonderfully confirmed in our own lives.

God does not always answer in just the way and at just the time we ask, of course, for He can see much further ahead than we can, and thus He does see that *"all things work together for good to them that love God, to them who are the called according to His purpose"* (Rom. 8:28). Of course there are conditions. We must pray unselfishly (James 4:3), without harboring and excusing some human sin in our lives (Ps. 66:18) and in accordance with His will (1 John 5:14–15).

But the bottom line is that the Lord *is* real, He *does* care, and He *does* answer prayer. When His answers involve a very unusual ordering of process rates or timing of events, though still within the framework of natural laws, we can realistically regard them as Grade B miracles, as the Bible does. Often we can rightly feel angels are involved in some way, even though God has not directly altered one of His laws to accomplish it.

Before I close this chapter, I would like to tell about one more instance of a Grade B miracle in my own life. My teaching experiences at Rice University during World War II, especially the joy of seeing many college students accept Christ and Christians grow strong in faith as a result of our campus Bible class and Christian fellowship there, had convinced me that teaching was what I was meant to do. That would, however, require going back to school for M.S. and Ph.D. degrees.

But I was married, with two children and a third on the way, so I would need to have a job to support the family. In those days, there were as yet no government fellowships or other financial aid, so I would have to do it on my own.

I wanted to major in hydraulics, with a minor in geology, as I felt that would be the best preparation for meaningful research in flood geology and creationism and also for a teaching career in water engineering (a branch of civil engineering, in which I already had a B.S. and several years of experience). The best program in the nation in this field was at the University of Minnesota and its famous St. Anthony Falls Hydraulics Laboratory. By God's grace, I was able to get a full-time instructorship there, teaching civil engineering courses and also doing sponsored research at the laboratory. We were able to get a one-year lease in a university faculty apartment complex, at a time (right after the war) when housing was in extremely short supply.

It was, indeed, an ideal arrangement, and I worked hard in my teaching and research assignments and in the two graduate courses I could schedule each quarter. We found a good church and also started a spiritually fruitful Bible class in the faculty apartments where we were living.

There was one real problem, however. Faculty salaries back in those days were notoriously low (more reasonable now!), and we were just barely getting by on my instructor's salary. We had no medical insurance, but had managed somehow to keep up with the obstetrician and other medical bills, as well as buying winter clothing and other necessities of life for us and our two children. But there was no way we could pay the hospital bill when the time would come for our third child to be born. We had moved to Minneapolis in August and the birth was scheduled for early December.

As it happened, John was born in the university hospital on December 7, 1946, the fifth anniversary of Pearl Harbor Day. My younger brother John had been killed in the war, so we thought it appropriate to name the baby in honor of his deceased uncle.

As the day arrived when we could have taken him home from the hospital, however, John's older brother and sister both came down with chicken pox, so the doctor insisted the baby remain in the hospital until they got well. Thus, the bill, already impossible for us to pay, kept getting bigger. Obviously, we were praying about this, but it seemed like some kind of loan was going to be mandatory.

But then — miraculously, I would say — a check arrived in the mail the day before we would be expected to take the baby home, and it was for almost the exact amount of the hospital bill!

The check was the first royalty payment on my first book, *That You Might Believe*, which had been written well over a year before, primarily for me to use in witnessing to the students at Rice. I had no idea this help might be coming, and the publisher had no knowledge of our urgent need at the time. But the Lord did!

All the circumstances surely precluded mere coincidence, and we naturally knew it was a rather remarkable answer to prayer — what I now would call a Grade B miracle.

I could recite many more examples in our lives, and probably many readers of this chapter could recite similar experiences in their own lives. God really does answer the earnest prayers of His family members — not always just when or how we would like, of course — but He does care and answer when we try to meet the biblical conditions; and sometimes the answers are so remarkable that we can call them at least Grade B miracles!

Then Pharaoh also called the wise
men and the sorcerers: now the magicians
of Egypt, they also did in like
manner with their enchantments.

(Exodus 7:11)

GOD WANTS TO BRING US BEYOND THE
POINT WHERE WE NEED SIGNS TO DISCERN
HIS GUIDING HAND. SATAN CANNOT
COUNTERFEIT THE PEACE OF
GOD OR THE LOVE OF GOD
DWELLING IN US. WHEN CHRIST'S
ABIDING PRESENCE BECOMES OUR GUIDE,
THEN GUIDANCE BECOMES AN ALMOST
UNCONSCIOUS RESPONSE TO THE GENTLE
MOVING OF HIS HOLY SPIRIT WITHIN US.

— BOB MUMFORD

CHAPTER VI

Counterfeit Miracles

L est we become too impressed with such reports of current-day miracles, we must not forget that Satan, the great deceiver, with his host of fallen angels (demons, evil spirits) is quite capable of producing some extremely impressive phenomena which look very much like miracles of providence (Grade B miracles), and perhaps even some that seem to be miracles of creation.

The Lord Jesus Christ said so himself, and said that these could have profound influence, especially during the last days. *"For there shall arise false Christs, and false prophets, and shall shew great signs and wonders; insomuch that, if it were possible, they shall deceive the very elect"* (Matt. 24:24).

Lying Wonders

But this is nothing new. The people of God had to be warned about such deceptive signs and wonders way back in Moses' day. Moses not only warned against such miracles, but indicated the deadly purpose behind them.

> *If there arise among you a prophet, or a dreamer of dreams, and giveth thee a sign or a wonder, And the sign or the wonder come to pass, whereof he spake unto thee, saying, Let us go after other gods, which thou hast not known, and let us serve them; Thou shalt not hearken unto the words of that prophet, or that dreamer of dreams: for the LORD your God proveth you, to know whether ye love the LORD your God with all your heart and with all your soul. Ye shall walk after the LORD your God, and fear him, and keep his commandments, and obey his voice, and ye shall serve him, and cleave unto him"* (Deut. 13:1–4).

The great miracles of Christ were at least in part designed to convince people that He was, indeed, *"the Son of the living God,"* so that through believing on Him people *"might have life through His name"* (John 20:31). Likewise, the deceptive counterfeits accomplished by false prophets were intended to persuade people to follow some false god or gods.

And it is sadly true that the many false religions of the world have all had their professed "prophets" and "miracle workers," and they have indeed been able to *"deceive many"* (Matt. 24:5, 11). The tremendously successful world religion called Islam, for example, has probably a billion adherents worldwide, all following the demonically inspired utterances of the so-called "prophet" Mohammed, undoubtedly the greatest of all the "false prophets" predicted by the Lord Jesus.

True or False — How to Tell

When the question arises as to how to distinguish a false prophecy or false miracle from those that truly are from God, the criterion given by Moses (see above) was the obvious test of purpose and motivation. That is, if the purpose was to persuade people to follow some other god or religion than the inspired revelation of the true God, then that is sufficient cause to reject it.

If the prediction made by the false prophet fails to come to pass, that is obviously adequate reason to reject his authority. *"When a prophet speaketh in the name of the LORD, if the thing follow not, nor come to pass, that is the thing which the LORD hath not spoken. . ."* (Deut. 18:22).

In the Israelite theocracy, such false prophecies were considered so dangerous as to warrant capital punishment. *"But the prophet, which shall presume to speak a word in my name, which I have not commanded him to speak, or that shall speak in the name of other gods, even that prophet shall die"* (Deut. 18:20).

Even if the miracle is real or if the prophecy does come to pass, that in itself is no proof that it was from God. As Moses said, if its purpose was to persuade people to go after other gods and follow their religion, it was at most allowed by God as a test of their devotion to the true God. In that case also, *"that prophet, or that dreamer of dreams, shall be put to death; because he hath spoken to turn you away from the LORD your God"* (Deut. 13:5).

Although such drastic action against false prophets or magicians is not warranted in Christian cultures today, there still exists a real danger of being turned away from Christ by these deceptive agents of Satan. Remember the warning of the apostle Paul that *"Satan himself"* can appear as *"an angel of light, Therefore it is no great thing if his ministers also be transformed as the ministers of righteousness"* (2 Cor. 11:14–15).

As noted in the preceding chapter, God's holy angels are often involved in what I have called Grade B miracles, or miracles of providence. While they cannot perform miracles of creation (only God is the Creator) they know much about God's natural processes and systems and how to control their timing or rate of occurrence. When appropriate or specially needed by those who are *"the heirs of salvation"* for whom they are *"sent to minister"* (Heb. 1:14), they can indeed accomplish *"signs and wonders"* and *"divers miracles"* as a witness to the validity of the message borne by the true disciples of Christ (Heb. 2:4).

The same is presumably true of the fallen angels at least to some degree — only they use such abilities not to further but to hinder the work of God through His disciples. Therefore, the apostle John has warned that we must always *"try the spirits whether they are of God: because many false prophets are gone out into the world"* (1 John 4:1).

As mentioned above, almost every religion has had its supposed miracles, prophecies, and means of direct communion with its "gods," and these are commonly cited by the adherents of that religion as evidence of its truth. But the real criterion of truth is its fidelity to the revealed, written Word of God, the Holy Bible.

In a time when God's people in Israel were being especially confused by professedly supernatural revelations and were in danger of following alien religions, the great prophet Isaiah brought a grave warning against such apostasy, in the following sober words:

> *And when they shall say unto you, Seek unto them that have familiar spirits, and unto wizards that peep, and that mutter: should not a people seek unto their God? for the living to the dead? To the law and to the testimony: if they speak not according to this word, it is because there is no light in them* (Isa. 8:19–20).

Regardless of how impressive a supposed miracle or supernatural revelation may appear to be, if it has been performed by a practitioner or holy man of Hinduism or Islam or any other non-Christian religion, offered as some kind of "proof" of that false belief system, it should instead be rejected as demonic in origin and satanic in purpose.

If this dictum seems harsh and unloving, we need to remember that the true Word of God is our authority. It would be more unloving to let those involved in such delusions think that we accept such phenomena as divine when we know they are not, thereby encouraging their adherents to continue therein. We need rather to try to deliver them from such deceptions if possible, doing so as graciously and lovingly as we are able.

If the question is raised as to how we know that the Bible (rather than the Koran or the Vedas or some other "holy" book) is the true Word of God, we must remind the doubters that this doctrine is what Jesus taught and that He verified His claim to be the only begotten Son of God by defeating death and rising from the dead. Thus, God *"hath appointed a day, in the which he will judge the world in righteousness by that man whom he hath ordained; whereof he hath given assurance unto all men, in that he hath raised him from the dead"* (Acts 17:31).

It is significant that the many great founders of other religious and philosophical systems all stayed dead once they died. Mohammed is dead, Buddha is dead, Confucius is dead, Zoroaster is dead, Lao-Tse is dead, Karl Marx is dead, Charles Darwin is dead, Mao is dead.

But our Lord Jesus Christ died and rose again by His own great power, alone of all men who ever lived *"I am he that liveth, and was dead,"* He said. *"And, behold, I am alive for evermore, Amen; and have the keys of hell and of death"* (Rev. 1:18). Furthermore, *"we have not followed cunningly devised fables"* (2 Pet. 1:16), for there are *"many infallible proofs"* of His bodily resurrection from the dead (Acts 1:3), the facts and exposition of which are found in many volumes and which provide the very foundation and explanation of Christianity.

We are well justified, therefore, in rejecting the testimony of these false prophecies and miracles found in the non-Christian religions (and even in certain pseudo-Christian cults). They may, indeed, be real signs and wonders in many cases, but the Bible calls them *"lying wonders"* (2 Thess. 2:9). Even though they may actually be "Grade B" miracles in some cases, their purpose is to deceive people into believing a lie — that is, that there is some other way of reaching heaven except through faith in Jesus Christ and His sacrificial blood shed on the cross to pay for our sins.

In fact, we American Christians no longer need special miracles or other supernatural signs to verify our Christian faith, for we have the complete Word of God — the Bible — and that's all we need. Remember that, on one occasion, Jesus himself rebuked the Jews who were asking Him to show them a miracle. *"An evil and adulterous generation seeketh after a sign; and there shall no sign be given to it, but the sign of the prophet Jonas: For as Jonas was three days and three nights in the whale's belly; so shall the Son of man be three days and three nights in the heart of the earth"* (Matt. 12:39–40).

He was referring, of course, to His coming death and resurrection, which has always been the crowning proof of both His deity and the saving mission on which He came to earth. We really need no other miraculous evidence — although, by God's grace, we do have an abundance.

During those early decades after His resurrection, while the first disciples were going out with the message of that mission, although they had seen the evidence of His resurrection first hand, their listeners needed more than just their personal testimony, and the New Testament itself was not yet available. Accordingly, *"God also [was] bearing them witness, both with signs and wonders, and divers miracles, and gifts of the Holy Ghost, according to His own* will" (Heb. 2:4).

The Temporary Gifts of the Spirit

The gifts of the Holy Spirit actually included certain supernatural abilities in some individual cases — *"gifts of healing . . . working of miracles . . . prophecy . . . divers kinds of tongues* [that is, ability to proclaim the gospel in foreign languages]…" (1 Cor. 12:9–10). These were of great value in starting to implement their great commission to spread the gospel to a generally hostile world.

Although the Holy Spirit still gives special gifts to believers to use in the church and the world, *"dividing to every man severally as He will"* (1 Cor. 12:11), it seems likely that the supernatural gifts were no longer given after they were no longer needed as a testimony to the truth of the gospel message. As Paul later wrote to the Corinthian believers who were tending to misuse some of these gifts, *"…whether there be prophecies, they shall fail* [same word as 'vanish away']*; whether there be tongues, they shall cease; whether there be knowledge, it shall vanish away. For we know in part, and we prophesy in part. But when that which is perfect is come, then that which is in part shall be done away"* (1 Cor. 13:8–10).

It seems rather clear (to me, at least) that the reason they only knew the truths of Christianity *"in part"* was because, although they did have some of Paul's teachings to guide them, they did not yet have the complete New Testament, and so were specially dependent on those members who had received the Spirit's gift of *"the word of knowledge"* and of *"prophecy"* and perhaps *"tongues"* to learn what they needed in the church and in their testimony to the world.

But these supernatural gifts would, in general, no longer be needed *"when that which is perfect is come,"* and so would be allowed to *"vanish away."* Once they had the complete and perfect written Word of God to guide them, they would no longer need instruction from those brethren who had such gifts. The New Testament books were all complete by the end of the first century, and they were all soon rapidly circulated to many of the churches (with many copies being made). There eventually would be no real need for miraculous gifts, but there could easily be a temptation to continue to display them ostentatiously, and so they were soon withdrawn. Even the gift of prophecy was replaced by the more permanently needed gift of teaching that which had already been revealed through the prophetic gift.

But this development may have given the evil spirits in the atmospheric heavens an increased opportunity to confuse and deceive through the use of counterfeit miracles and false prophecies — *"lying wonders."* Actually, such phenomena have been present in pagan religions since long before the Christian era. Sorcerers, witches, magicians of various sorts, witch doctors, necromancers, and the like abounded in ancient times and have continued ever since. God, through Moses, made these to be capital crimes among His chosen people. And the miraculous gifts of the Holy Spirit in the early church obviously provided an incentive for demonic imitation as a means of infiltrating and corrupting the Christian testimony.

Satan has always been an imitator and deceiver, not a creator, and the same is true of his agents. They could not create the ability to speak in foreign tongues, but they could imitate this gift by inducing people to mutter impressive gibberish: indeed, this practice has occurred in certain Islamic sects and other groups, ancient and modern, with no Christian connection at all. While they cannot foresee the distant future, they can (presumably through demonic network-ing) correctly anticipate certain short-range events and thereby make some channelers appear to be true prophets. Long-range predictions, however, must be couched in vague symbolic ramblings that can be arbitrarily interpreted to have prophesied whatever later happenings may actually occur.

Satan is, of course, brilliantly cunning and knows much about human physiology and psychology. Thus, so-called "divine healers" have been prominent in practically every non-Christian religion. Furthermore, the phenomenon of demonic possession is apparently very real today, as reported by many missionaries and other Christian workers, just as it was in the time when Jesus and the Apostles repeat-edly had to deal with that problem.

This all means that Satan and his angelic/demonic followers are able to counterfeit (not duplicate, but imitate) the working of the true Spirit of Christ and his various gifts to men. That is probably one reason, at least, why the miraculous gifts of the Holy Spirit were mostly withdrawn after they had served their purpose and the New Testament was complete and available.

Satan also has the ability to influence human minds, especially those that are not truly yielded to the Holy Spirit's control (which, of course, is always fully in accord with Scripture). Thus, as Peter re-buked a Christian who was seeking unjustified praise from his fellow believers, he said, *"Ananias, why hath Satan filled thine heart to lie to the Holy Ghost . . . ?"* (Acts 5:3).

A similar statement is made in Scripture concerning Judas and his decision to betray Jesus: *"the devil having now put into the heart of Judas Iscariot, Simon's son, to betray him"* (John 13:2). Sinful acts usually have their origin in sinful thoughts or temptations. Not all of these come directly from the devil, of course. *"But every man is tempted, when he is drawn away of his own lust, and enticed. Then when lust hath conceived, it bringeth forth sin"* (James 1:14–15).

However, some temptations (as in the case of Judas mentioned above) do come directly from Satan or one of his agents. So Peter warns that *"your adversary the devil, as a roaring lion, walketh about, seeking whom he may devour"* (1 Pet. 5:8). And Paul urges us to *"be renewed in the spirit of your mind. . . . Neither give place to the devil"* (Eph. 4:23–27).

The point is that Satan and his demonic angels do have the ability, when they deem it worth their while, to influence our minds and our thoughts away from God and His Christ. This evidently includes the ability to deceive us even into thinking that a thought or an act — perhaps even a miracle — is from God even when it is really from Satan. That is why Christ warned about those false prophets who could show *"great signs, and wonders"* attempting to *"deceive the very elect"* (Matt. 24:24).

They can even induce hallucinations in the minds of certain available subjects, causing them to think they are seeing or hearing things they are not. The classic biblical example occurred at the court of Pharaoh in Egypt, who was being petitioned by Moses to let the Israelite slaves go free. When Moses' rod miraculously became a serpent, the king's court sorcerers seemed to turn their rods into serpents also.

That could not really be, however, because only God can create life. He is the living God. *"For as the Father hath life in himself, so hath he given to the Son to have life in himself"* (John 5:26). Satan was a created being, like all other creatures, including angels. We have to conclude, therefore, that these miracles of Pharaoh's magicians were counterfeit miracles, *"lying wonders,"* accomplished by mental trickery, perhaps some form of hypnotism, induced hallucinations in Pharaoh and his courtiers.

There is no doubt that the Bible recognizes that Satan can produce a great variety of deceptive *"signs and wonders"* for the purpose of drawing men away from the true God to some other man or religion, with the probable ultimate purpose of getting them to accept him (Satan, or Lucifer) as the one true sovereign god of the universe. These counterfeit miracles could never be miracles of creation (what I call Grade A miracles), but might well be very impressive Grade B"miracles — not creating anything but manipulating the processes and systems that God had created in such a way as to appear to produce miraculous events of some kind.

But how is one to know the difference? Christ said that some of their counterfeits might even deceive the very elect, if possible.

But the answer is simple enough. If they do not exalt the deity of Christ, as well as His perfect humanity, or *"if they speak not according to this Word, it is because there is no light in them"* (Isa. 8:20). The Bible itself — the written Word of God — is the test. Not any new "revelation" by some self-claimed prophet or guru, not any new "discovery" of humanistic (or even deistic) science or philosophy, not any "reinterpretation" of the plain teachings of Scripture. Just the Bible, taken literally except when the context indicates some (always easily understood) figurative meaning. The Bible is the Word of God, verbally and fully inspired and authoritative. That is all we need for discernment, but that is essential.

And the priests that bare the ark of the
covenant of the Lord stood firm on the ground
in the midst of Jordan, and all the Israelites
passed over on dry ground, until all the people
were passed clean over Jordan.

(*Joshua 3:17*)

"I BELIEVE IN GOD THE FATHER ALMIGHTY, MAKER OF
HEAVEN AND EARTH." WHAT DOES THIS MEAN? I BELIEVE
THAT GOD HAS MADE ME AND ALL CREATURES; THAT HE HAS
GIVEN AND STILL PRESERVES TO ME MY BODY AND SOUL, EYES,
EARS, AND ALL MY MEMBERS, MY REASON AND ALL MY SENSES;
ALSO CLOTHING AND SHOES, MEAT AND DRINK, HOUSE AND
HOME, WIFE AND CHILD, LAND, CATTLE AND ALL MY GOODS;
THAT HE RICHLY AND DAILY PROVIDES ME WITH ALL THAT I
NEED FOR THIS BODY AND LIFE, PROTECTS ME AGAINST ALL
DANGER AND GUARDS AND KEEPS ME FROM ALL EVIL; AND
ALL THIS PURELY OUT OF FATHERLY, DIVINE GOODNESS AND
MERCY, WITHOUT MERIT OR WORTHINESS IN ME; FOR ALL OF
WHICH I AM IN DUTY BOUND TO THANK AND PRAISE, TO
SERVE AND OBEY HIM.

— MARTIN LUTHER, 1483–1546

CHAPTER VII

Grade A Miracles and the Bible

Despite the pronouncements of the scientific establishment, real supernatural miracles *have* occurred — Grade A miracles, miracles of creation, miracles in which one or both of the two supposedly universal laws of thermodynamics had to be temporarily set aside. To insist that such miracles are impossible, as David Hume and many others have done, is equivalent to atheism. For if God does exist, He established the laws of "nature"

in the first place. Since He is, by definition, omniscient and omnipotent, He certainly can suspend or modify His created laws when and if He chooses to do so.

The question is not: *Can* miracles really happen? The question is: *Do* they happen? And *that* is a question of historical evidence, not science.

God is not capricious, of course. He does not perform miracles just for show, or to satisfy the ego of some self-professed miracle-man or divine healer or whatnot. His laws are good laws and we can be sure that, when one of them is momentarily suspended, there is some overwhelmingly good reason to do so.

Uniformity in the Present World

When the terrible flood of Noah's day was finished, God had said: *"While the earth remaineth, seedtime and harvest, and cold and heat, and summer and winter, and day and night shall not cease"* (Gen. 8:22). That is, the most basic constants of nature (the orbital revolution of the earth around the sun, and the rotation of the earth on its axis) which control or influence practically all other natural processes would not be ever changed again, as long as the earth itself remained. Basic uniformity would characterize the world and all its processes, from then on.

This situation would not preclude occasional miracles, of course, but the general picture would be one of essential worldwide uniformity of natural laws and processes until the very end times.

This had not been the case *before* the Flood. The two great events of creation and the Flood were non-uniform in the extreme. The same was true of the Fall and God's resultant curse on Adam and all his dominion. In effect, the end of creation week introduced the first law of thermodynamics, the Curse established the second law, and then the Flood was followed by the imposition of basic uniformity on the operation of all natural processes operating *within* the two laws.

That's the way the world operates now, except in occasional miracles. The biblical record tells of many events which could be called Grade B miracles, or miracles of providence, and this kind of miracle occurs today as well.

Grade A miracles, requiring the direct creative activity of God, are also recorded fairly often in the Bible, though they are extremely rare today. These are now considered scientifically impossible, but they *have happened*, especially during biblical days.

Criteria of Authenticity of Miracle Reports

As mentioned above, the question is not whether they can happen (science says no) but whether they did happen (history says yes). There are two historical criteria which they would need to satisfy to be considered real. One is whether or not God had adequate reason to set aside one of His basic laws; the other is whether or not the actual historical evidence is strong enough to show that He really did do so. And the fact is that all the Grade A miracles of the Bible abundantly satisfy both criteria. They really did happen!

For example, consider the long day of Joshua, certainly one of the most difficult to believe from a naturalistic point of view. According to the account in the Bible, this occurred very soon after the Israelite multitude had entered the promised land of Canaan. They had crossed the Jordan and conquered the ancient city of Jericho, two events which had also been facilitated by miracles. The Jordan River, which had been overflowing its banks, suddenly stopped flowing at all, *"and all the Israelites passed over on dry ground"* (Josh. 3:17).

It is possible that this could have been a Grade B miracle, naturalistically accomplished by a damming of the flow by a sudden landslide far upstream, so that *"the waters which came down from above stood and rose up upon an heap"* (Josh. 3:16). If so, one might assume that the landslide itself (which is believed by some workers to have been partly confirmed by archaeology) had been triggered by angelic encouragement.

Then the walled city of Jericho was conquered by Joshua's forces when *"the wall fell down flat, so that the people went up into the city, every man straight before him, and they took the city"* (Josh. 6:20).

This miracle (which, though the dating is controversial, seems to have been partially confirmed archaeologically) may also have been a Grade B miracle, accomplished by a providentially timed earthquake. Once the walls had crumbled, the pagan defenders of Jericho were no match for the Israelites, who proceeded to destroy its inhabitants and burn the city.

But then they had to face a confederation of Amorite armies. The Amorites were the dominant tribe among all the Canaanites that inhabited the Promised Land, and they would have to be defeated before the Children of Israel could inhabit the land promised to their fathers.

When Abraham had first been given the promise, God told him that since *"the iniquity of the Amorites was not yet full"* (Gen. 15:16), they would have to wait another four hundred years to receive its actual fulfillment.

The Long Day

But by Moses' time, it *was* full, the Israelites had grown into a powerful army, and it was finally time to displace the ungodly Amorites. Joshua soon put the Amorite confederation to flight, but God had instructed that they should be destroyed completely, and it became clear that they could not finish that job in the one afternoon remaining.

Therefore, Joshua prayed and then (evidently after being so instructed by the Lord), *"he said in the sight of Israel, Sun, stand thou still upon Gibeon; and thou, Moon, in the valley of Ajalon. And the sun stood still, and the moon stayed, until the people had avenged themselves upon their enemies. . . . So the sun stood still in the midst of heaven, and hasted not to go down about a whole day. And there was no day like that before it or after it"* (Josh. 10:12–14).

This was, indeed, an amazing miracle. Some writers have attempted to devise quasi-naturalistic ways of explaining it, but none have even come close to doing so. That the earth had to stop rotating and the moon to stop in its orbiting the earth is indicated by the fact that *both* the sun and the moon stopped and stayed where they were in the sky for about a whole day.

Some skeptics have objected that such an event would have caused great tectonic disturbances all over the earth. The obvious reply to that, of course, is that the God who could stop the whole earth from rotating could also prevent any disruptive movements on its surface. Actually, if the earth were *gradually* decelerated to a stop, there would probably not even have been any tendency for such surface displacements. There might well be an effect on the atmosphere or subsurface lavas, however, and this might be a proximate explanation of how *"the LORD cast down great stones from heaven upon them"* at the same time.

But how do we know that this amazing event really happened? Bible skeptics, of course, reject it automatically as a fanciful story that never really occurred at all.

I noted earlier that two criteria should be applied to reports of any alleged Grade A miracle. The first, that involving an adequate reason for God to suspend or change one of His laws (in this case, creating a special force that could slow and stop the earth from rotating and the moon from orbiting) is abundantly satisfied. This was the beginning of the fulfillment of His promise to Abraham. If the Amorites had been able to escape and later organize the armies of all the other Amorites and Canaanites to fight Joshua, the Israelites might well have been destroyed or driven back into the wilderness.

Another reason would be to demonstrate to the sun-worshiping, moon-worshiping, nature-worshiping Canaanites — as well as the Israelites themselves — that the God of Israel controlled the sun and moon and all the forces of nature. Most of all, He showed again that He was indeed the Creator and could control His creation and keep His word.

As far as evidence is concerned, the very fact that it is recorded in the written Word of God is sufficient evidence for me (it is also mentioned later in Hab. 3:11).

Some later scribe, however, apparently inserted the editorial note: *"Is not this written in the book of Jasher?"* in the middle of Joshua 10:13, perhaps in response to the assertion of the skeptics of his day that such an event could never happen. The book of Jasher (possibly meaning "Upright") seems to have been a continuing record of the great deeds of the righteous judges and other leaders of the Israelites over several generations (it is also mentioned in 2 Sam. 1:18).

There are practically no other written records surviving from that early date (about 1400 B.C.). However, there are many ancient legends of a long day (or long night in the western hemisphere) that have come down from ancient nations. One of the best collections of these is in the provocative book *Worlds in Collision*, written by the atheist Immanuel Velikovsky. Another was in a book called *Bible Myths* by T.W. Doane.

In any case, there is certainly good reason to accept the biblical record of the long day as true history, originally written by Joshua himself, who was *there!* The fact that he prayed for the sun to "stand still" instead of the earth was certainly no basis for calling him unscientific, as some modern skeptics have done. Modern-day astronomers, surveyors, and navigators use exactly the same sort of terminology (the fully scientific terminology of "relative motion") when they speak of the movements of the heavenly bodies.

In any case, we can certainly accept the historicity of the long day, as well as that of all the other biblical miracles. There is always an adequate rationale and adequate evidence to warrant us in doing so.

Crossing the Red Sea

Another amazing miracle, completely impossible to explain on any naturalistic basis, was the parting of the Red Sea to enable the Children of Israel to cross over on dry land and thus to escape Pharaoh's pursuing army, as described by Moses in the 14th chapter of Exodus. The various quasi-naturalistic compromises that have been suggested in relation to this unique event all founder on verse 22. *"And the children of Israel went into the midst of the sea upon the dry ground: and the waters were a wall unto them on their right hand, and on their left."*

This was clearly supernatural, a Grade A miracle requiring creation of some kind of anti-gravitational energy to sustain the two walls from collapsing. There obviously was an urgent reason for such divine interference: the very survival of God's chosen people.

In fact, the very existence of Israel, continuing through all the centuries since this mighty miracle, is itself evidence of the historicity of the miracle. Israel would not even be here otherwise.

Furthermore, in addition to the Mosaic account, the Red Sea crossing is often eulogized in later biblical passages (Ps. 106, 136, 66, 78; Neh. 9; Isa. 43, 51), and even in the New Testament by Stephen (Acts 7:36), by Paul (1 Cor. 10:1, 2), and the writer of Hebrews (11:29). There is no doubt that all the people of Israel regarded it as a real event, the great miracle that became the foundation of their nation. It is even mentioned in at least one of the apocryphal books (*Wisdom of Solomon* 19:7).

There is no point in commenting on the other great miracles of the Old Testament. The long day and the Red Sea crossing are probably the hardest to believe, except for the creation of the universe itself and then the great world-destroying flood in the days of Noah. But many volumes have already been published by many scholars defending the historicity of these two latter unique events, and some of the basic evidence for them has been discussed in chapter III.

The evidence for creation and the Flood, of course, is so compellingly strong that the apostle Peter cites these two events as the conclusive answer to scoffers who reject the very possibility of miracles. When they insist that *"all things continue as they were from the beginning of the creation,"* thus asserting the universal prevalence of naturalism, he calls them *"willingly ignorant"* of the primeval creation of the heavens and the earth *"by the word of God,"* followed later by the great cataclysm when *"the world that then was, being overflowed with water, perished"* (see 2 Pet. 3:4–6).

In fact, it has been truly said that, if a person *really* believes Genesis 1:1 — that is, that God *created* the heavens and the earth — he should have no trouble believing any of the other miracles of the Bible. If God really created all things, He certainly controls all those things. Thus, for a man to deny the possibility of true supernatural miracles is equivalent to announcing that he is an atheist, and in view of all the evidence that is there if he just looks, the Bible says he is a *"fool"* (Ps. 14:1; 53:1; Rom. 1:21–22), and *"without excuse"* (Rom. 1:20).

The Grade A miracles of the Bible all really happened, just as recorded. There was a good reason for each of them, and adequate evidence confirming them. Those skeptics who deny them and those liberal theologians who try to devise rationalistic explanations for them (such as arguing that Christ's feeding of the five thousand was accomplished by persuading the people to share with each other) are *"willingly ignorant"* and *"without excuse."*

I have tried to list all the Grade A miracles of the Bible (from both the Old and New Testaments) in an appendix in my book *The Biblical Basis for Modern Science* (also as an appendix in my *Defender's Study Bible*). According to my count, there are 232 specific miracles listed in the Bible, but only 38 percent of these are creation miracles

(Grade A). Fifty-five percent are providential (Grade B) and 7 percent demonic.

These figures are tentative and approximate, of course. I certainly could have missed some or placed some in the wrong category. But they are at least indicative. Obviously, true supernatural miracles were extremely rare, even in biblical times, with only 89 recorded during more than 4,000 years of human history, thus averaging only one every 45 years. Furthermore, a large portion of these occurred in three clusters, during the ministries of Moses, Elijah/Elisha, and Christ, respectively.

Providential miracles are somewhat more frequent in the Bible but, as discussed previously, these can and do occur fairly often even today. Demonic miracles (Grade B type, but aided by the working of fallen angels instead of the ministry of God's faithful angels) occur very rarely, but do seem to be increasing in frequency today, and we need to be sober and vigilant. Remember the warning of the Lord that their lying signs and wonders can almost deceive the very elect.

I want to discuss true providential miracles a little more in the last chapter. In general, real Grade A miracles are very rare today, requiring as they do God's direct intervention in His basic laws of conservation and decay. These laws, and the innumerable natural processes which operate within them, are good for almost every situation and are being upheld by Christ himself (Heb. 1:3; Acts 17:28; Col. 1:17).

It is also true that Paul wrote that prophecies, tongues, and probably other supernatural gifts would cease, presumably after the last apostle had died and the Bible had been completely inscripturated (1 Cor. 13:8–10; Eph. 3:3–5).

However, in context, this curtailing of the miraculous specifically referred to the gifts of the Spirit, not to special miracles such as had been accomplished in the Old Testament and in the personal ministry of Christ before the Spirit began to bestow His particular gifts on individual Christians. The Spirit still does that, of course, but His gifts today are appropriate for the post-apostolic church, now that the whole Bible is complete and not to be changed in any way (Rev. 22:18–19).

Grade A miracles were rare, even in biblical times, and are even more so today. But they can occur when there is an urgent need and occasion, and when God so wills.

The Miracle of Regeneration

There is one Grade A miracle, as mentioned earlier, which does occur often today and, in fact, has been occurring frequently throughout the Christian era. This is the miracle of individual regeneration.

> *Therefore if any man be in Christ, he is a new creature: old things are passed away; behold, all things are become new. And all things are of God, who hath reconciled us to himself by Jesus Christ* (2 Cor. 5:17–18).

This, indeed, is a marvelous work of divine creation ("creation" is the same as "creature" in the Greek).

Here is a person who was *"dead in trespasses and sins"* who has suddenly been *"quickened"* (that is, "made alive") *"together with Christ, (by grace ye are saved")* (Eph. 2:1–5). He has been *"born again,"* this time not by natural human birth, but *"born of the Spirit"* (John 3:3, 8), and his whole life, especially his heart, has been changed. He has been delivered *"from the power of darkness"* and *"translated"* into the kingdom of God's Son, *"in whom we have redemption through His blood, even the forgiveness of sins"* (Col. 1:13–14). God had made Christ *"to be sin"* for him, that he *"might be made the righteousness of God in* [Christ]*"* (2 Cor. 5:21). Like all true Christians, he has been saved by God's grace through faith in Christ, and *"created in Christ Jesus unto good works"* (Eph. 2:10).

Note the fact that he has been *created* in Christ, and is thus a new *creation* in Him. His old life has passed away and a new life begun. He has been newly created by God, and thus the laws of thermodynamics have been in his case displaced by *"the law of the Spirit of life in Christ Jesus"* (Rom. 8:2).

This is surely a Grade A miracle in the truest sense of the word. He had been going down to everlasting death and hell, but now is on the way to heaven and eternal life with the Lord. This miracle of creation happens frequently, whenever a person truly turns to Christ for forgiveness and salvation. I experienced *this* Grade A miracle, long ago — and I hope it has happened (or will soon happen) to you as well.

He is not here: for he is risen,

as he said.

Come, see the place

where the Lord lay.

(Matthew 28:6)

Filling the world

He lies in a manger.

— Saint Augustine of Hippo, 354–430

CHAPTER VIII

The Greatest Miracles

In a small book such as this it would not be feasible to discuss *each* of the miracles of the Bible, but there is one special group of miracles on which the Bible itself places special emphasis. These are the seven great "signs" (meaning "miracles") described in the gospel of John and there referred to in the climactic passage of that book, as follows:

And many other signs truly did Jesus in the presence of His disciples, which are not written in this book: But these are written, that ye might believe that Jesus is the Christ, the Son of God; and that believing ye might have life through His name (John 20:30–31).

The word translated here as "signs" is the Greek *semeion*, which is translated "sign" or "signs" 51 times, as well as "miracle" or "miracles" 22 times. The miracles of Christ were not mere marvels to make an impression, but were actual *signs* sent from heaven to vindicate His claims and demonstrate His deity. As Israel's greatest teacher of that age, Nicodemus acknowledged, *"No man can do these miracles that thou doest, except God be with him"* (John 3:2).

More or less incidentally, each of these great miracles also met some specific human need, but its main purpose was to show that the man Jesus was actually the eternal Son of God. He is indeed able to give eternal life to all who believe on Him as not only the long-anticipated Messiah of the Jews but as the redeeming Son of the living God, able to save their souls forever.

The Seven Miracles

John tells us that his own real purpose in writing his gospel was evangelistic, not just historical. He could best accomplish this mission by demonstrating the deity of the man Jesus. And *that* demonstration could best be achieved by centering his narrative around seven of Christ's most significant miracles as signs proving His deity. These seven can be listed as follows:

(1) Transmuting water into wine (John 2:1–11)

(2) Healing a dying son six miles away by merely speaking a word (John 4:46–54)

(3) Providing sound limbs for a man crippled for 38 years (John 5:1–16)

(4) Feeding a vast multitude with two loaves and five small fishes (John 6:1–14)

(5) Walking on the stormy Sea of Tiberias (same as Galilee) (John 6:15–21)

(6) Providing new eyes for a man who had been blind all his life (John 9:1–7)

(7) Raising a man back to life after four days in the grave (John 11:1–44)

One can quickly note that these seven miracles were all utterly supernatural, with no realistic way of explaining them as mere coincidences or even as statistical marvels. Each required the special creative power of God and thus is what I have called a Grade A miracle. They were evidently selected as representative (seven being the number of fulness) out of the scores of miracles that Christ had performed, for the very purpose of leading men to Christ.

It is not surprising that John's gospel has been more used in soul-winning than any other book of the Bible. John, in fact, stated that this was his purpose in writing it — not only hoping to win his Jewish compatriots but also the Gentiles among whom he was ministering. It is worth noting in passing that John began his evangelistic gospel with a strong passage on creation (John 1:1–9), then proceeded to the human incarnation of the Creator (John 1:10–18) and His sacrificial death for the sin of the world (John 1:29–36). This is an ideal model and outline for our own witnessing for Christ.

But we do need to take a brief look at each of the seven miracles, noting how each was a Grade A miracle, demonstrating the deity of Christ, while at the same time meeting a specific human need.

First, Jesus transformed the simple molecular structure of water into the much more complex structure of new wine, thus meeting a supposed crisis at a marriage feast at the request of his mother, thereby setting aside and reversing the second law of thermodynamics. Incidentally, we note that the wine He created was *new* wine, not old, intoxicating wine. The wedding guests were already drunk after exhausting the initial wine supply (they had *"well drunk,"* according to John 2:10, where the Greek word for "well drunk" means literally "drink to intoxication"), yet Jesus provided them with about 150 gallons of new wine! Old, fermented wine is, of course, a decay product, being produced in conformity to the second law. Jesus, who condemned drunkenness (e.g., Luke 21:34) would certainly never do anything to cause a drunken crowd to become even more intoxicated! Those who use this miracle to justify their drinking practice are sadly mistaking its main purpose, which was to manifest *"His glory"* and to cause *"His disciples"* to believe on Him (John 2:11).

The second miracle described by John was to heal a nobleman's son over in Capernaum, even though Jesus at the time was in Cana, at least six miles away. He merely spoke a word of assurance, the son was healed, and the nobleman believed (John 4:50). Jesus thus again reversed the action of the second law and also demonstrated the mighty power of His mere word. He did not touch the man's son, nor even see or hear him, but merely spoke, *"for His word was with power"* (Luke 4:32).

Third, Jesus miraculously transformed the hopelessly crippled limbs of a man who had been in that state for 38 long years. The man *"immediately . . . was made whole"* (John 5:9). Since his limbs had been altogether atrophied, the Lord must have actually *created* new limbs for him, overcoming the first law of thermodynamics to do so.

The fourth great miracle described by John involved the actual creation of matter, despite the otherwise universal law of conservation of matter. There were *"about five thousand"* men, apparently not counting the many women and children, that were fed from only *"five barley loaves, and two small fishes"* (John 6:9–10). And then the disciples *"filled twelve baskets with the fragments of the five barley loaves, which remained over and above unto them that had eaten"* (John 6:13).

That same evening, the Lord Jesus must have created some kind of anti-gravitational energy, and He was thereby able to walk on top of the waters of the storming Sea of Galilee to reach His disciples who were desperately trying to row to the other side of the lake. When He reached them *"they willingly received Him into the ship: and immediately the ship was at the land whither they went"* (John 6:21). Evidently He had walked across the entire width of the Sea of Galilee while it was fiercely raging and while the disciples were having great difficulty in rowing the same distance. Thus, in one day He had created both matter and energy, despite the restrictions imposed by His first law of thermodynamics, His law of conservation of matter and energy.

The sixth miracle was that of providing good eyes for *"a man which was blind from his birth"* (John 9:1). This was a direct creation of both matter and complexity, superseding both laws of thermodynamics. When the Pharisees interrogated the man and then reviled him for giving Jesus the credit, *"The man answered and said unto them, Why herein is a marvelous thing, that ye know not from whence He is, and yet He hath opened mine eyes. . . . Since the world began was it not heard that any man opened the eyes of one that was born blind. If this man were not of God, He could do nothing"* (John 9:30–33).

Indeed this *was* a tremendous Grade A miracle, with the incidental confirmation that such miracles are extremely rare. Has anyone ever encountered a person with the alleged "gift of healings," who could provide perfect eyes for a person blind from birth?

But probably even greater than this was the seventh miracle in John's gospel, when Jesus raised his friend Lazarus from the dead, after *"he had lain in the grave four days already"* (John 11:17). Even though Lazarus had been buried properly, with all the appropriate grave clothes and ointments, corruption had already set in (John 11:39). Jesus could call him forth, not only from the tomb, but his spirit even from Hades.

As the account says: *"He cried with a loud voice, Lazarus, come forth. And he that was dead came forth"* (John 11:43–44). Lazarus even joined Jesus and his sisters for a supper in the home of Mary and Martha several days later. Soon the priests were planning to put Lazarus to death again, because this amazing miracle had resulted in a real problem for them. For, *"by reason of him many of the Jews went away, and believed on Jesus"* (John 12:11).

Note again that each of these seven great miracles featured by John was a Grade A miracle in the fullest sense, requiring the power of the Creator himself to accomplish. In each case, one or both of the two universal laws of thermodynamics had to be set aside for a still higher law.

Also, note that each of these miracles was seen by many people — never by, say, a handful of credulous believers in a darkened room somewhere. Each met a specific human need as well, but John's specific reason for selecting these seven to write about (only two of which had even been mentioned in the other three gospels, all written earlier) was *"that ye might believe that Jesus is the Christ, the Son of God; and that believing ye might have life through His name"* (John 20:31). Yet there was still one more miracle after these, greater by far than any of them.

The Resurrection of Christ

The greatest miracles since the creation of the universe, of course, have been the incarnation, death, and resurrection of its Creator. The miraculous conception and virgin birth of Christ constitute another wonderful miracle of creation, and His substitutionary death a miracle of providence, when He volitionally died at a time of His own choosing.

But then, on the third day, He arose from the dead and left the tomb where His body had lain. In His resurrection body, He appeared to His grieving disciples, *"To whom also he shewed himself alive after his passion by many infallible proofs, being seen of them forty days, and speaking of the things pertaining to the kingdom of God"* (Acts 1:3).

There are at least ten such occasions recorded in the New Testament when He showed himself during those 40 days to one or more of His followers, including one time to a gathering of at least 500 of them (1 Cor. 15:6). Then, much later, He appeared again to John, this time in His glorified body, making this amazing claim:

> *Fear not, I am the first and the last: I am he that liveth,*
> *and was dead; and, behold, I am alive for evermore, Amen;*
> *and have the keys of hell and death* (Rev. 1:17–18).

Without this greatest of miracles, there would have been no Christianity at all, and men would still be lost in their sins, alienated forever from God. *"Because I live,"* said Jesus, *"ye shall live also"* (John 14:19).

It is noteworthy that, in the very first sermon preached after the Resurrection, the climactic part of Peter's message was:

> *This Jesus hath God raised up, whereof we all are wit-*
> *nesses. . . . Know assuredly, that God hath made that same*
> *Jesus, whom ye have crucified, both Lord and Christ. . . .*
> *Repent, and be baptized every one of you in the name of Jesus*
> *Christ for the remission of sins* (Acts 2:32– 38).

Great numbers of people did respond on that occasion, as well as later, as Peter and the others continued to preach about the resurrection. *"And with great power gave the apostles witness of the resurrection of the Lord Jesus. . . . And daily in the temple, and in every house, they ceased not to teach and preach Jesus Christ"* (Acts 4:33–5:42).

The apostle Paul, of course, also centered his preaching around the Resurrection, with his classic written discussion in 1 Corinthians 15. Among other points, he there stresses the fact that *"if Christ be not risen, then is our preaching vain, and your faith is also vain. . . . And if Christ be not raised, ye are yet in your sins"* (1 Cor. 15:14–17).

And, as Paul wrote to the Romans, Christ has been *"declared to be the Son of God with power . . . by the resurrection from the dead"* (Rom. 1:4). In his very last epistle, Paul urged his young pastoral disciple that in his preaching he must *"Remember that Jesus Christ . . . was raised from the dead according to my gospel"* (2 Tim. 2:8).

Thus, the very existence of Christianity is a witness to the truth of the Resurrection and the fact that those first disciples were willing to die for that truth.

And *why* were they so sure? Well, they had seen Him, heard Him speak, touched Him, eaten with Him. They were skeptical at first, but then they had to acknowledge the *"many infallible proofs"* by which He had shown that He was alive — intimate one-on-one conversations with some, several meetings with the whole group of His closest followers, plus at least one with over 500. In no way could these have been mass hallucinations of some kind, nor could they all have been mistaken about His identity, having seen the nail prints in His hands and the spear scar in His side. Nor was it some kind of spectral appearance; they could touch Him and see Him eat.

He had only showed himself to His own followers, however, so the others who had rejected Him diligently tried to manufacture various reasons not to believe. The Romans had moved His body, the body had been stolen by His disciples, He had not really died but merely swooned, it was all a plot to form a new cult, His followers missed Him so much that they merely deluded themselves into thinking He had been raised — whatever absurd tale they could come up with to avoid believing that He had really defeated death and emerged vibrantly alive from the tomb.

However, every one of these stratagems soon foundered on the fact that His tomb was empty, and the body could not be found. When multitudes began responding to the gospel and the preaching of the Resurrection, the authorities (both secular and religious) began to do all they could to stop this spreading flame of salvation through Christ. Since this whole turning to Christ was based on His resurrection, all they would have needed to do, of course, was to locate and exhibit the body, and that would quickly have doused the flame.

But that they could not do! The body which they sought had indeed been raised from the dead and, by the time these mass conversions were taking place (even many of the priests had become Christians, as we are told in Acts 6:7), He had already been taken up into heaven, where the Son of God, now incarnate as the God-man, was seated at the right hand of the Father. They could not reach His body there! All they could do was try to stop the spread of this belief by persecuting its followers.

That, however, only served to give further evidence that it was true. It soon became obvious to everyone that the only remaining escape from the truth of the Resurrection was to assume that the whole thing was a monstrous plot, and that Jesus' dead body had been hidden away somewhere by these conniving disciples. This was soon recognized as an impossible scenario, of course, for no conspiracy can prosper when its followers are being impoverished and executed for preaching something they all *knew* to be false! Men may be willing to die for preaching some strange doctrine they passionately believe to be true — but *never* for a cause they know is based on a flat-out lie! Some things just can't be.

Not only the original 12 apostles but all their followers were soon swept up in the persecutions of the Jewish priests and the Roman emperors — yet they never tried to escape by deciding and confessing that it had all been a great conspiracy. The evidence to the believers had become so overwhelming that they simply had to believe in Christ and His resurrection, no matter how much such a stand would cost them.

This very brief analysis can only scratch the surface of this evidence. Many volumes have been written on the evidence for the bodily resurrection of the Lord Jesus Christ and, although many have tried, none have ever been able to refute it. A fair number of skeptical scholars who have begun their study of this subject with the very purpose of refuting the evidence have, in the course of their investigations, been converted themselves. Furthermore, many top-rate historians and legal minds have concluded that the bodily resurrection of Jesus Christ is at least as firmly proved as any fact of history.

The validating evidence for this supreme miracle of the Christian faith is so unanswerably genuine that it not only confirms the deity of Christ, but, indirectly, all the other miracles of the Bible and the Bible itself as a miracle book. That is what Jesus believed and taught,

and He is the eternal Son of God and the Creator and sustainer of life. We do well to believe what He believed, as well as all that He has said.

And when she knew Peter's voice,
she opened not the gate for gladness,
but ran in, and told how Peter
stood before the gate.
(Acts 12:14)

TRUE PRAYERS ARE LIKE CARRIER PIGEONS:
FROM HEAVEN THEY CAME, THEY ARE ONLY
GOING HOME.

— CHARLES HADDON SPURGEON, 1834–1892

CHAPTER IX

Prayer and Providence

I have called Grade B miracles — the kind that clearly do happen occasionally today — miracles of providence. They may not require special acts of divine creation, but do involve such improbable combinations of time and process as to suggest some kinds of explanation other than accidental coincidence. The possibility of angelic manipulation of these processes and circumstances, in their ministry to the human heirs of salvation, has also been stressed.

As stressed earlier, Grade A miracles, requiring the supernatural creative power of God himself, are certainly very rare, and any such alleged supernatural miracle must certainly require a very clear reason for God to interfere in His universal (and good) laws of conservation and decay, as well as incontrovertible evidence that He has actually done so. They should also be such as to support true biblical Christianity (not counterfeit miracles, such as can be performed by Satan and his host of fallen angels, or demons, designed to lead people away from that truth).

The Necessary Rarity of Creation Miracles

That such miracles of creation are at least extremely rare today is evident from the fact that many sound, sincerely Bible-believing pastors and teachers are convinced that they never occur at all, and probably ceased soon after the apostolic period.

I also agree with many Bible teachers that the individual miraculous gifts of the Holy Spirit (that is, gifts of healings, prophecies, foreign languages, etc.) probably ceased soon after the completion of the New Testament Scriptures (as convincingly foretold by Paul in 1 Corinthians 13:8–10). But this does not mean we should regard all supernatural miracles as never occurring today, even when the criteria have been satisfied for recognizing them. God is still omnipotent and is well able to answer prayer, when it is His will to do so; He created His so-called laws of science and is well able to change them when He so wills.

Miracles are rare today, of course, even Grade B miracles. God's basic laws of nature are good laws, and there must always be a good reason to supersede them, whether for a nation or an individual. If they were commonplace events, performed at the bidding of a magician, they would hardly be considered divine miracles. The possibility of counterfeit miracles might be examined, as Satan and his angels are often able to produce what the Bible calls lying wonders in order to deceive the unwary and turn them to some false religion.

More often, however, such frequent "miracles" really turn out to be natural processes after all, once their phenomena have been carefully and scientifically investigated.

The Post-Flood Natural Order

As mentioned previously, Genesis 8:22 is a key verse in prescribing the general uniformity and reliability of natural processes in today's world. After the terrible deluge, which destroyed every air-breathing land animal on the earth (except those in Noah's ark), along with multitudes of marine animals, then God promised Noah He would never send such a cataclysm again.

> *While the earth remaineth, seedtime and harvest, and*
> *cold and heat, and summer and winter, and day and night*
> *shall not cease* (Gen. 8:22).

That is, God was assuring Noah and his descendants that the most basic geophysical controls would be constant from then on. That is, the rotation of the earth on its axis and its distance from the sun (which control the regularity of day and night), along with its orbital revolution about the sun and its inclination on its axis (which control the length of its year and the succession of seasons) would henceforth be uniform as long as the earth would last.

This would of necessity assure the essential uniformity of most other terrestrial processes — the hydrologic cycle, the atmospheric circulation, vegetal growth, etc. — which are all essentially determined and controlled by the earth's rotation and orbital revolution. Perhaps this implied that this had *not* been the case during the Flood itself (the length of the year, for example, seems to have been changed by the Flood, from 12 months of 30 days each to the present annual cycle of 365+ days, with months arbitrarily divided in length as well.

We have already noted that the two basic laws of conservation and decay began at the time when God completed His work of creation (Gen. 2:1–3) and when He pronounced the Curse on His creation because of Adam's sin (Gen. 3:17–19), respectively. Here then was His enunciation of a third global principle, the essential uniformity of natural processes functioning within those two laws.

This very stability of nature's processes is itself a testimony to God's providential care for His creation. Otherwise, chaos would reign everywhere and science would be impossible. The very nature of things would make it impossible for man to obey God's primeval mandate to "subdue" and "have dominion" over the earth, with all its living creatures and physical systems. As it is, this "dominion mandate" (Gen. 1:26, 28) authorizes the development of science, technology, and all other human vocations to use in our exercising our divinely given stewardship under God over His creation.

The tragedy is that this stewardship has been misused in two ways. Some have made it into a despotism, abusing earth's creatures and its environment instead of properly caring for them as stewards. Instead of studying and developing its resources for the benefit of mankind and the glory of God, many have despoiled them in the name of greed and power. But God has warned that He will *"destroy them which destroy the earth"* (Rev. 11:18).

Then there are many men who, in the name of science and all its benefits, have made God's very laws and processes into a god. They have, in effect, *"changed the truth of God into a lie, and worshipped and served the [creation] more than the Creator"* (Rom. 1:25). Unless they repent, God gives them up as well (note Rom. 1:26, 28).

That such attitudes will be especially characteristic of the last days was noted by the apostle Peter in the very last chapter he wrote, just before his martyrdom. Here it is:

> *. . . there will come in the last days scoffers . . . saying, Where is the promise of his coming? For since the fathers fell asleep, all things continue as they were from the beginning of the creation* (2 Pet. 3:3–4).

This is essentially nothing less than a restated form of God's promise to Noah (Gen. 8:22), as cited above — except instead of being accepted as God's gracious assurance of nature's reliability as men tried to carry out His dominion mandate, they had corrupted it into a boastful assumption of nature's independence of God and therefore of their own supremacy over the creation, since they themselves were apparently the highest systems evolved by that creation. In worshiping the creation, they were really worshiping themselves. They had decided that *"all things continue as they were,"* and thus there was no possibility of miracles, especially any supernatural intervention of God at some future consummation of history.

Evolution out of Nothing

They could not even acknowledge that there must have been a supernatural *beginning* of the laws and processes they were worshiping, since they maintained that all things had continued naturalistically since the very *beginning* of that creation! That is, somehow the creation had created itself!

This absurdity is actually the belief of the self-professed leaders of physical cosmology today. The originator of the inflationary model of the origin of the universe, accepted today by the great majority of modern cosmologists, astronomers, and physicists, is Alan Guth, professor at MIT. He has said, "So, in the inflationary theory the universe evolves from essentially nothing at all, which is why I frequently refer to it as the ultimate free lunch" ("Cooking Up a Cosmos," *Astronomy*, September 1997, p. 54).

This strange cosmology is a remarkable testimony to man's desperate attempt to escape God, as well as a remarkable fulfillment of Peter's prophecy. As we have seen, the two laws of thermodynamics inexorably point to the conclusion that, although the universe must have been created at some time in the past, it could *not* have created itself!

Modern scientists, as typically represented by Dr. Guth, must simply ignore these universal laws if they want to deny God. Yet Guth has the gall to say that "we are approaching a scenario for the creation of the universe that is compatible with the laws of physics" (as cited in "*Guth's Grand Guess*" by Brad Lemley in *Discover*, April 2002, p. 38). But then, when asked how he accounts for the laws of physics, he simply says, "We are a long way from being able to answer that one" (Ibid).

No we're not! The Creator established them when He finished His work of creating all things and then later placed them under the curse of decay because of man's sin. Guth, of course, does not believe this answer, but he has nothing else to offer, and neither does any other scientist anywhere. No wonder Peter says that those who insist that *"all things continue as they were from the beginning of the creation"* are guilty of willful ignorance (2 Pet. 3:4)!

Not only are miracles possible, but the two greatest physical miracles — creation and the Flood — are the two key facts of earth history, both supported by an overwhelming abundance of evidence. Yet, just as Peter prophesied, these are the very facts that the last-day scoffers, *"willingly are ignorant of, that by the word of God the heavens were of old, and the earth standing out of the water and in the water: Whereby the world that then was, being overflowed with water, perished"* (2 Pet. 3:5–6).

The evidence of creation and the Flood (briefly surveyed in chapter III) has been documented copiously and need not be repeated here. There are now literally thousands of fully qualified scientists who — in this present generation — have abandoned evolutionism and uniformitarianism and returned to literal biblical creationism. You can be sure they *"have not followed cunningly devised fables"* (2 Pet. 1:16), but have had to resist powerful scientific peer pressure and sometimes even loss of employment to do so. They are well able, as Peter urges, *"to give an answer to every man that asketh you a reason of the hope that is in you"* concerning why they believe such unpopular truths (1 Pet. 3:15).

Since God surely exists, there is no valid reason to deny either the historical reality of the miracles described in the Bible or the possibility of miracles occurring today. With respect to the latter, the question is not their possibility but their actuality. As stressed earlier, this is essentially a question of the adequacy of divine purpose and the adequacy of human testimony.

To have a Grade A miracle today, one or both of the two universal scientific laws of thermodynamics would have to be overcome, and these are powerful and good laws. One would need to be able to cite overwhelming divine reason and human witness for such a claim to be convincing. Possible, but rare! Except for the miracle of regeneration, of course.

Grade B miracles, on the other hand, while not everyday affairs, have undoubtedly occurred and do occur in the modern world from time to time. I have cited several in the lives of people I have known, as well as in my own life, and could cite a considerable number of others if necessary. Such miracles do not break any *law* of science, but may involve extremely unusual rates or locations or times of processes operating within the laws. It is usually possible to discern a good reason for the Lord to arrange such a miracle when one does occur, and sometimes there are even indications of angels working the contributing factors (rate, timing, etc.) as part of their ministry to the heirs of salvation, adjusting the normal uniformity of processes (as announced in Gen. 8:22) to make it all come together.

The fact that the basic processes work at constant rates (e.g., earth rotation, moon's revolution, etc.) does not mean that each of the innumerable dependent processes (rainfall, plant growth, etc.) must also be rigidly constant. As noted previously and as is obvious, these process rates are variable within limits, though usually the long-term averages are fairly constant.

It would probably be hard to pinpoint exactly how wide a variation from the average a particular process or circumstance would have to show before the event affected thereby would be called a Grade B miracle. No doubt judgment and experience would come into play. One person's miracle might be merely an unusual coincidence to another. Of course, if it were *known* that angels had been involved, then there should be no doubt.

Providential but Sad

One very sad (but no doubt providential) experience in our family comes to mind. Our youngest son, Andy, was only 39 when the Lord took him to heaven. He had recently received a Ph.D. degree from Texas Tech and had served two years as an assistant professor at Florida State University when he was suddenly stricken with cancer in his lymph system in February of 1989. Despite intensive chemotherapy treatments, which did not really seem to help at all, his body deteriorated quickly and he died in May, leaving a beautiful wife and three young children.

They had been attending Tallahassee's First Baptist Church and were apparently much loved there, for the pastors and members were frequent visitors in his hospital room, and many prayed for him there. Also, many of his faculty colleagues and graduate students came, and he faithfully tried to witness to them. When the cancer got so bad he could not talk clearly, he wrote out a testimony and had each visitor read it when they came.

All of this made quite an impression on a 90-year old Roman Catholic patient in the room across the hall. He began to pray earnestly, asking God to take him and spare Andy, since his own useful life was past and Andy's best years should be ahead of him. Andy died a few days later, with only his wife at his bed. She said he was asleep, but she could actually sense when his spirit left the body. He had left a taped message for each of his three children and his wife, and these served as his goodbyes.

But then one of the church pastors told me a remarkable story. While he was visiting a day or so before, he felt he should call on the old Catholic man across the hall. The latter gave a clear Christian testimony, and then told him how he had been fervently praying for God to take him instead of Andy, when, he said, he suddenly saw an angel standing by his bed. The angel told him that God had heard his prayers, but that He could not do as he had requested, because God had other plans for Andy now.

I do not understand all this, and cannot personally verify it. But this was how the account came to me, and I have to believe it because otherwise it seems impossible to me to make sense out of Andy's very sudden physical disintegration and death.

That all took place in the spring of 1989, which was 14 years ago as of this writing. The family he left behind has had many difficult times since then, but the Lord has always provided their needs, and all of them are sincere and unquestioning believers in the Lord Jesus.

I am well aware that other Christian families have experienced some wonderful answers to prayer in times of great need, and even of the presence of ministering angels in certain unusual and stressful circumstances. Ours is not the only family that can relate such testimonies. Such miracles are rare at best, of course, even providential, Grade B miracles.

But that does not mean that answers to prayer are rare! Jesus taught that *"Men ought always to pray"* (Luke 18:1), and Paul said that we should be *"instant in prayer"* (Rom. 12:12). Such admonitions would be pointless if He did not intend to act on these prayers (or, perhaps, assign designated angels to do so).

Prayer and Grade C Miracles

In fact, the entire life and ministry of a true believing Christian could be considered as one ongoing and continuing answer to prayer. The provision of daily material needs and daily guidance and innumerable other concerns, in response to daily prayer (both regular and as-needed prayer) is a marvelous reality for the Christian.

There are many, many books that have been written on prayer, of course, and there is no need to discuss this subject in depth here. As mentioned earlier and as Christians are well aware, there are certain conditions attached (faith, unselfishness, no known unconfessed sin, good relationship with one's spouse, etc.) along with the understanding that God's will is paramount and that God's answer can be in the negative or long delayed if that is better in His sight.

I am sure that every mature Christian would acknowledge that God does answer prayer. The answers are often general answers to general prayers, but sometimes specific answers to specific prayers. In any case, we do pray and God does answer, and then we pray in thankfulness. Sometimes the answer seems long delayed (such as praying for an unsaved loved one for many years), but then the answer finally comes, possibly even after the death of the one praying. All prayer, of course, must be answered according to God's will and wisdom.

So perhaps these ought also to be considered miracles. They do not require the breaking of a law of science, nor any extreme variation in the statistics, so are neither Grade A nor Grade B miracles. But they do involve God's intervention in response to the prayer. Could we acknowledge these normal answers to normal prayers as Grade C miracles? Why not?

God's providential leading in a Christian's life is so clearly evident (at least to him or her) that to recount its many manifestations would sound like boasting. But it is not that — it is simply a testimony of God answering prayer throughout the days as He has promised to do. Such a normal Christian life could thus well be described as an ongoing series of Grade C miracles.

And once in a while, if there is a very urgent need or unique set of circumstances, one of these might turn out to be a Grade B miracle (even possibly, though unlikely, Grade A). We must always remember that "*. . . with God nothing shall be impossible*" (Luke 1:37), and that He "*is able to do exceeding abundantly above all that we ask or think, according to the power that worketh in us*" (Eph. 3:20). Therefore, as Paul exhorts, let us "*Continue in prayer, and watch in the same with thanksgiving*" (Col. 4:2).

ℱurther ℛeading

This list is not intended as a complete bibliography, but only as a guide to a few of the more comprehensive and relevant studies of miracles, for any who wish to pursue the subject further.

Herbert Lockyer, *All the Miracles of the Bible* (Grand Rapids, MI: Zondervan Publishing House, 1961), 34 pages. This is a very comprehensive and reverent exposition of each of the biblical miracles. It also contains a substantial bibliography on the subject.

Ernest Gordon, *The Fact of Miracle* (Francestown, NH: Marshall Jones Co., 1955), 126 pages. A unique study of numerous reported miracles in the post-apostolic centuries. However, the incidents include many occult miracles, as well as those in professedly Christian contexts, and in most cases have little or no verification of the veracity of the reports.

Ada R. Habershon, *The Study of Miracles* (Grand Rapids, MI: Kregel Publications, 1957), 336 pages. A reprint of a classic study by a very gifted 19th century Bible teacher.

C. H. Spurgeon, *The Miracles of Our Lord* (London: Marshall, Morgan and Scott, 1959). A reprint of a classic study by the "prince of preachers," dealing specifically with the miracles of Christ.

Henry M. Morris, *The Biblical Basis for Modern Science,* second edition (Green Forest, AR: Master Books, 2002), 474 pages. See, especially, pages 17–86, 433–438. Contains appendices listing all the Bible's miracles of creation, miracles of providence, and demonic miracles.

INDEX

INDEX OF SCRIPTURES

Other books by Henry M. Morris

THE BEGINNING OF THE WORLD
A thorough explanation of the first eleven chapters of Genesis, the most contested chapters in the Bible. In a format that can be used for Bible studies.
ISBN: 0-89051-162-4 • 184 pages • $8.99

THE BIBLE HAS THE ANSWER
How do we know the Bible is true? How will we spend eternity? Here is a complete resource to these and other tough questions.
ISBN: 0-89051-018-0 • 394 pages • $11.99

THE BIBLICAL BASIS FOR MODERN SCIENCE
The most detailed analysis of all aspects of creation/evolution. Includes illustrations, charts, etc., plus expositions of twelve major scientific disciplines.
ISBN: 0-89051-369-4 • 300 pages • $13.99

BIBLICAL CREATIONISM
This unique book discusses every passage in the Bible that deals with creation or the Flood.
ISBN: 0-89051-293-0 • 280 pages • $12.99

CHRISTIAN EDUCATION FOR THE REAL WORLD
A thoroughly biblical approach to education in the world today, based on over 50 years experience in teaching and educational administration.
ISBN: 0-89051-160-8 • 296 pages • $10.99

CREATION AND THE SECOND COMING
Dr. Morris goes back to the beginning to unveil the details and events of our future. He begins the prophetic countdown at creation and reveals many fresh insights into Scripture.
ISBN: 0-89051-163-2 • 194 pages • $10.99

DEFENDING THE FAITH
Shows Christians the danger in compromising with a philosophy like evolution. Offers a fresh look at Satan's age-old war agains God and the harmful effects it has had on society.
ISBN: 0-89051-324-4 • 224 pages • $11.99

GOD AND THE NATIONS
Dr. Morris examines the history of nations in light of biblical history, and looks at the future of the nations in biblical prophecy.
ISBN: 0-89051-389-9 • 176 pages • $10.99

Other books by Henry M. Morris

THE GOD WHO IS REAL
Helps Christians with some of the philosophical objections seekers have when confronted with the gospel. Contrasts other faiths with the true path, by pointing to the God of special creation.
ISBN: 0-89051-299-X • 126 pages • $9.99

THE LONG WAR AGAINST GOD
Thoroughly documents the fact that the idea of evolution did not originate with Darwin — it is basic in ancient and modern ethnic religions and in all forms of pantheism.
ISBN: 0-89051-291-4 • 344 pages • $13.99

MANY INFALLIBLE PROOFS
Widely used as a textbook, many consider this to be the most useful book available on the whole scope of Christian evidences and practical apologetics.
ISBN: 0-89051-005-9 • 400 pages • $11.99

MEN OF SCIENCE, MEN OF GOD
101 mini-biographies of great Bible-believing scientists of the past, many of whom were the "founding fathers" of modern science.
ISBN: 0-89051-080-6 • 107 pages • $7.99

THE MODERN CREATION TRILOGY (3-volume set)
Produced by Dr. Morris and son, Dr. John Morris, this set looks at the creation/evolution issue from three main aspects: Scripture, science, and society. Gift-boxed set includes CD-ROM
ISBN: 0-89051-216-7 • 232, 343, & 208 pages • $34.99

101 SIGNS OF DESIGN . . .
TIMELESS TRUTHS FROM THE WORD
This pocket-sized book from the series highlights quotations from Dr. Morris.
ISBN: 0-89051-366-X • 112 pages • $4.99

THE REMARKABLE JOURNEY OF JONAH
One of the most intriguing and controversial books of the Bible is the story of Jonah. Was he real? Was the "great fish" real? Readers will find their faith strengthened by the reality of Jonah's life, and the lessons he has for all of us.
ISBN: 0-89051-407-0 • 144 pages • $9.99

Other books by Henry M. Morris

THE REMARKABLE RECORD OF JOB
The Book of Job is a revelation of God and His creation, presented here as an amazing scientific record that provides clues to the great flood of Noah and the dinosaurs.
ISBN: 0-89051-292-2 • 146 pages • $8.99

THE REMARKABLE WISDOM OF SOLOMON

A verse-by-verse commentary on the Books of Proverbs, Ecclesiastes, and Song of Solomon, also includes much research and detail about the life of Solomon.
ISBN: 0-89051-356-2 • 240 pages • $11.99

SCIENTIFIC CREATIONISM
An excellent reference handbook on important creationist viewpoints of history and science, easily understood by readers with non-scientific backgrounds.
ISBN: 0-89051-003-2 • 284 pages • $10.99

THAT THEIR WORDS MAY BE USED AGAINST THEM

The most complete guide to evolutionists' quotes available. Contradictory statements made by evolutionists in various scientific fields.
ISBN: 0-89051-228-0 • 500 pages • $21.95

TREASURES IN THE PSALMS
Can be used as a devotional, as it focuses on the spritual, physical, and scientific dimensions of the Psalms, including insights not commonly taught.
ISBN: 0-89051-298-1 • 408 pages • $13.99

WHAT IS CREATION SCIENCE?

Perfect for pastors, parents, and instructors, as well as the science student, great evidence is shown for design in both physical and biological sciences. Written with Dr. Gary Parker.
ISBN: 0-89051-081-4 • 336 pages • $11.99

WHEN CHRISTIANS ROAMED THE EARTH
A powerful collection of essays, including work by Dr. Morris, discusses UFOs, Noah's flood, the decline of the modern church, the effects of evolution on the culture, and cavement.
ISBN: 0-89051-319-8 • 224 pages • $11.99